The Books of a New Nation

*United States Government
Publications, 1774–1814*

PUBLICATIONS OF THE
A. S. W. ROSENBACH FELLOWSHIP IN BIBLIOGRAPHY

EXAMPLES OF HOUSE AND
SENATE PRINTING
(From the Collections of Mrs. Joseph Carson)

House Journals of the Fifth Congress, first session (the daily issues printed by William Ross, delivered in pamphlet form, stitched); a Senate bill in its second reading, a committee report, and a Senate resolution, all from John Fenno's shop, are examples of several different kinds of printing ordered by the Clerk of the House and the Secretary of the Senate in 1797. Such copies as these, in their original condition, not bound into volumes, are rare today.

The Books of a New Nation

United States Government Publications, 1774–1814

by

J. H. POWELL

*A. S. W. Rosenbach Fellow
in Bibliography, 1956*

Philadelphia
University of Pennsylvania Press

To—

"There exist no sources of historical information in a free and enlightened country, so rich and so valuable, as its publick journals, and the proceedings and debates of its publick bodies and associations."

—PETER FORCE

"This Government, sir, has its foundations in the public will; and if we wish it to strike deep into public affection, and to be cherished and upheld, the public must understand not only its operations of today, but its history."

—Congressman JOHN DAVIS of
Massachusetts, 1831

Contents

printing activities in the late 1790's . . .
Summary of practices and conditions in the
year 1800.

Publication problems raised by the government's move to Washington City . . . Printers in the new capital . . . Question of the
first Washington government imprint . . .
Sketch of Samuel Allyne Otis, Secretary of
the Senate . . . His relations with William
Duane . . . John Beckley, Clerk of the House
. . . Roger Chew Weightman succeeds to
the Senate Printing . . . Otis and Weightman: an era in government printing . . .
Issues and problems before the reconstruction of the city and the government after
1816.

Illustrations

The Books of a New Nation

United States Government
Publications, 1774–1814

1

Novus Ordo Seclorum

TWENTY-FIVE YEARS AGO, MR. CHRISTOPHER MORLEY WAS presented here as the first A. S. W. Rosenbach Fellow in Bibliography. In the five lectures he gave, he launched this series of annual exercises in the study and enjoyment of books with such spirited flourishes of charm, taste, and relish that this platform has been an uneasy place ever since for those on whom, as an accolade, the responsibility of following him has been conferred.

Mr. Morley called his lectures *Ex Libris Carissimis*— "out of the best-loved books"—which is exactly the sort of title that should be used in association with the name Rosenbach, and it makes a happy sound in the colorful, anecdotal fraternity of collectors.

Now, on the twenty-fifth anniversary of this Fellowship, I propose to speak, not as did Mr. Morley of the magic worlds of Conrad, DeFoe, Stevenson, DeQuincey, not of the perfumes and odors of treasured rarities, but of the Published Documents of the United States Government, most of which are, alas! books no collector esteems, and bibliographers have not studied. To pore over stiff broadsides, statutes of Congress, fiscal accounts, departmental and committee reports, court cases, treaties, Senate and House journals, military orderings, import schedules, forms of land warrants, and the like is not the most beguiling pursuit in American Studies, I admit. Dr. Rosenbach once wrote, "After love—I say, *after* love—book collecting is the most exhilarating sport of all." [1] I know he was not thinking of government documents when he shaped that careful sentence. And indeed it has occurred to me, from the way the public printing of the nation has been neglected, that in succession to Mr. Morley I might well entitle my wreath of dry leaves, *Ex Libris Minus Æstimatis*—"out of the least-noticed books"—thus warning you fairly that we have grim, serious antiquarian business in hand, which bookmen, more used to the amenities of their pursuit, may find less a pleasure than a penance.

Yet the subject is not entirely lacking in that special kind of charm which belongs to books. I do not mean to lay a deceptive veneer over the tough subject matter I have to deal with, but the great charters and organic instruments of our government are, after all, included in it. And there are actually items, even minor ones, which tell the sort of story collectors love. One such item belonged to Dr. Rosenbach, and enthusiastically he described it. The British admiral, Sir George Cockburn, while the men he commanded were setting their fires in the capitol building in Washington that August day, 1814, looked around the president's office for a souvenir of the dreadful occasion he had ordered. He picked up a book, and took it with him. It was a thin folio, bound in marbled paper over boards, with a leather spine strip. On the front was pasted a green morocco label, bearing the legend in gold letters, "Presi-

dent of the U. States." Later, in a more leisurely moment, the admiral opened the book and wrote in it,
"Taken in the President's room in the Capitol, at the
destruction of that building by the British, on the cap-
ture of Washington 24th August 1814 by Admiral Cockburn and by him presented to his eldest brother Sir
James Cockburn of Langton, Bart, Governor of Ber-
muda." Dr. Rosenbach was very proud of this treasure.[2]
I wish I might add that the book on President Madison's
desk had been a classical text on the fall of princes, or
an original Convention printing of the Federal Constitution of the "U. States" with Madison's *marginalia*.
It was not. The book so narrowly snatched from the
burning was entitled, I regret to say, *An Account of the
Receipts and Expenditures of the United States, for the
Year 1810. Stated in pursuance of the standing order of
the House of Representatives of the United States,
passed on the thirtieth day of December, one thousand
seven hundred and ninety-one. Washington: A. & G.
Way, Printers. 1812.*
Government documents are all too likely to have
merciless titles like that—*Accounts of Receipts and Expenditures*—and to have texts which reveal nothing beyond the mere artisanship of statecraft. From the collector's point of view, from the literary, from the aes-
thetic, let them burn, unless the admiral himself has
rescued and inscribed them.
But there is that one thing, that "mere artisanship
of statecraft," the inner workings of the viscera of government, which the documents reveal. This is why I have
chosen the subject: to see whether the bibliographical
study of the United States government as publisher,

during its first forty years, can help the historian understand how, from the meeting together of a few likeminded men in protest in 1774, there emerged, without prior plan, three elements new in our political life: The first, a primitive but nonetheless actual and functioning government over and in addition to the governments of the several colonial commonwealths; the second, a set of political principles, a series of big words— *union, nation, liberty, rights, sovereignty*—which enlarged the scope, the ambit of this new government in the everyday living of Americans; the third, a more skilled, complete, and competent administrative machinery, by the development of which the national government became indeed the government of a nation, adequate in its inner processes to effectuate those principles which were the reasons for its enlarging and persisting, long after the original necessities that first called it into being had ceased to exist.

I have taken the titles for my three problems from one of the government documents of the period. It is, perhaps, unfortunate that the titles are in Latin, for they are peculiarly American phrases. The document in which they appear is—at least, I hope it is—familiar to you all: you see it every day, on the reverse side of the one-dollar bill. It is the Great Seal of the United States, the sign-manual of our sovereignty as a nation, which after six years of intermittent discussion was adopted by Congress on June 20, 1782, and with only minor changes has remained our official device ever since. On the Great Seal, which was jointly the product of two Philadelphians, William Barton the scientist and Charles Thomson of Harriton, Secretary to the Continental

Congress, are the three mottoes of our nation, chosen
by Thomson. The first, *novus ordo seclorum,* "a new
order of the ages," refers to the year of Independence,
1776. Thomson adapted it from the fourth *Eclogue* of
Vergil, fifth verse. I use it to designate the period 1774–
89, when a new government called itself into being and
developed its various functions. The second, *e pluribus
unum,* "out of many, one arises," had long been the
motto on the masthead of the *Gentleman's Magazine,*
a British periodical read regularly by many American
subscribers. To me it seems the perfect phrase to designate the years 1787–1800, when the new, stronger federal government formed in Convention began to unify
the administrative structure of the nation. The third,
annuit coeptis, Thomson found in Vergil's *Æneid,* book
ix, verse 625; it occurs again in the *Georgics,* I, 40. By
it he meant God—the all-seeing Eye of Eternal Providence pictured on the Great Seal—had favored our undertakings. By using it for the period 1800–14, I mean
to imply that when, after ten years in New York and
Philadelphia, the American government moved to
Washington City, it had learned how to operate; administrative practices had developed into successful governmental routines.[3]

Now the enquiries I raise are more historical than
bibliographical problems, perhaps; but bibliography
can help solve them in essential ways. This is only the
second time in twenty-five years that the A. S. W. Rosenbach Fellowship in Bibliography has been committed
to a person whose study has been entirely confined to
the fields of history.[4] From time to time I have been
impressed by the unfortunate separation between these

two disciplines. And while I am prepared to agree with the late Randolph Adams that historians generally neglect bibliography and sometimes scorn the pursuit of rare books, that the collector, the bibliophile in America has often *preceded* the scholar, and bibliographers have illuminated dark areas of our past that historians have not yet explored, still I must also observe that there is another side to this shield: there are numerous problems that historians have raised in all seriousness for which they require the assistance of the bibliographer but can find only an inadequate bibliographical literature to support them.

It is a genuine handicap to the historian that there exists no single, authoritative bibliography of the literature of the American Revolution. Though a great many special studies have been made, they are so scattered through whole shelves of books and journals that we may properly say the systematic bibliographical recording and analysis of the literature of our birth as a nation is yet to be prepared. Similarly, United States published documents is such an unharvested crop.

Indeed, if bibliographers had ever discovered in themselves the same lively enthusiasm for the printing history of the American government that they have shown for, say, the periodical parts of Dickens' novels or the various "points" of a first *Huckleberry Finn,* we should be much further along by now than we are in our humanistic understanding of ourselves as a free and democratical people, and of those elements in our politics that shaped the ideals and habits by which we still live. We need a quantitative study, listing just exactly what the government published each year, which would

demonstrate in simple graphic terms the development
of the federal structure from 1774 through the disaster
of "Mr. Madison's War." We need qualitative, textual
investigations, tracing not only the development of the
power to govern and the means of governing, but describing also the activities governed—the expansion of
the government into new areas of subject matter each
decade, even each year. The exact authorship of our
basic charters, laws, and instruments, as they emerged
from committee deliberations, needs to be investigated
and established, and the sometimes hidden authorship
of our presidential messages and proclamations.[5] What
Mr. Julian Boyd has brilliantly shown us can be done for
the public documents in which Jefferson had a hand [6]
should be done for all the emissions of the Congress and
departments. And the specialized bibliographical problems of the printing contracts, who the printers were,
how they were paid, what committees dealt with them
and what officials, what the effect of government contracts was on the history of the printing trade, would
furnish ample matter for numerous quarterly journals
and numerous Rosenbach lectureships.

America, Prince Metternich said, was a nation which
set idols against idols and thrones against thrones. How,
except by the creation of a government new in the manner and the matter of its undertakings, new in the atti-
tude that government's place was to serve, not dominate
the lives of its people? Yet for some reason the bibliography of our government has never appealed to
scholars. There is an aridity about the subject, perhaps;
yet there is drama, too, in that hopeful excitement that
greeted the government's emergence and first steps as a

novel, uncertain experiment in human welfare, a drama not entirely lost even today as we contemplate the far-from-novel or experimental behemoth into which that government has grown.

Now in speaking this way of the needs in the field, I do not mean to show a disregard for such work as has been done. There has been quite a lot of it, but most of it is not bibliographical; much of that portion which is bibliographical was not done by trained bibliographers; and the few trained bibliographers who did touch the subject proved singularly obtuse about the basic problems of government documents. The *American State Papers,* thirty-eight volumes published from 1832 to 1861 covering the years 1789 to 1833, were reprints of noncurrent materials existing in various offices of the government. The principal compiler, whose name is nowhere mentioned as editor in the whole series, was General William Hickey, chief clerk to the Secretary of the Senate during all those years. General Hickey was the leading authority of his time on federal documents, but he left no other records of his knowledge than his great compilation of 2,464 State Papers.

Peter Force had a fine historical enthusiasm but only moderate knowledge of his field. His interest was never bibliographical, and never centered on official imprints of the government. Still, had not Secretary of State Marcy killed his great project of *American Archives* by his complete lack of interest, Force's collections might have grown from the nine volumes that were actually published into the great monument he originally envisioned.

Congressman Ben Perley Poore actually did wheel a barrel of apples across a state, to pay an election bet when Millard Fillmore failed to carry Massachusetts. He was that kind of a man. His *Descriptive Catalogue* of 1885, though all libraries use it, is neither descriptive nor a very good catalogue, and he included in his ill-made lists items that had never even been published. He should have done better. Historical and bibliographical sciences by 1885 were both far enough advanced to persuade us that almost anyone could have done better.

The greatest landmark, for the historian, in early American documents bibliography came in 1900, again not from a bibliographer, but in this case it scarcely mattered. Even though experts find things to say to its disadvantage, *Public Documents of the First Fourteen Congresses, 1789–1817*, by A. W. Greely, remains the best and the basic bibliographical work in the field it covers. By any standards, it is an amazing achievement to have been wrought by one man. But then by any standards, Adolphus Washington Greely was an amazing man. He deserves our attention. He has recently received far too little.

One day in March, 1936, the Secretary of War, who was an individual named George M. Dern, escorted by a formidable troop of the military in parade dress and appropriate units of music, appeared on a quiet street in Georgetown. While the soldiers took stiff positions outside, the Secretary disappeared into a modest house, and with such formality as he could muster in a parlor he read before an ancient, elegant, bushy-bearded Yankee a citation of wonderful deeds of courage long ago, and presented to General Greely the Congressional Medal of Honor. The General chuckled. And he made a few remarks, which began something like this: "Well, I guess they've changed their minds about me." On his ninety-first birthday, a man is likely to say anything.

A. W. Greely spent seventy-four years and a bit in the Army. He was only sixteen in 1861, but he was accepted in a Massachusetts brigade as a private. He came from old Bay-State families, Mayflower descendants, Greelys, Cobbs, the Ingersolls of Salem, the Clements of Haverhill. Oliver Wendell Holmes, the justice, was in his brigade. They started together, served the whole war together, were both wounded three times. At Antietam, Greely was shot in the face; struggling to his feet, he took another bullet in his thigh. He was in many battles, was commissioned, commanded a company of Negro volunteers, ended the war as a brevet major.

He stayed in the Army, with the rank of second lieutenant of Infantry. In 1867 he was assigned to the Signal Corps; in 1873 he was made first lieutenant of Cavalry. He supervised the building of two thousand miles of telegraph lines in Texas, the Dakotas, California, and Montana. He was still first lieutenant in 1881 when he was given command of the American part of a famous International Polar Expedition, to Lady Franklin Bay. On the iron-clad whaler *Proteus,* with twenty-four other men in his command, he broke through the ice of Kane Basin, set up his subpolar post Fort Conger, made elaborate scientific observations, explored Grant Land and Grinnell Land, discovered lakes and fjords; he penetrated to latitude 83:24—farther north than any other human being had ever been. Then came disaster. The relief ship was two years behind schedule. In a fantastic Odyssey of horror, all but six of the twenty-five in the expedition died of starvation, exposure, and scurvy. Greely ate his sealskin gloves, his boots; somehow he survived. The man who rescued him was Admiral Schley.

When he came back "from up there, out of the world for three years," he found he had been demoted, through the political influence of others. Foreign nations decorated him, America did not. Still he remained in the Army, in the Signal Corps, where he conducted the Weather Bureau. He was made captain in 1886; suddenly the next spring, 1887, President Cleveland appointed him Brigadier General and Chief Signal Officer of the Army. He was the first volunteer soldier ever to reach the rank of general in the Regular Army. As Chief Signal Officer, Greely wrote a good deal on weather— technical studies: *Diurnal Fluctuations of Atmospheric Pressure;* economic studies: *Climate of Nebraska,* of New Mexico, of Texas, and Colorado and Utah too; conservation studies: *Irrigation and Water Storage in Arid Regions;* Arctic studies: *Chronological List of the Auroras.* And he wrote a general book on weather: *American Weather. A Popular Exposition.* It was still being used as a textbook at Harvard thirty years later.

But the Arctic was his love, and his two-volume report of his expedition to Lady Franklin Bay was his first published document in the Signal Office. He wrote other books on the Arctic, on explorers and travelers, on Alaska, on weather of the far north. All his life he kept writing, more than a hundred books all together, typed them out himself with one finger of each hand. His *Handbook of Polar Discoveries* went through five editions, his *Alaska* through three; in his eighty-fourth year he wrote his autobiography, in his eighty-fifth he published *The Polar Regions in the Twentieth Century* ("The entire public may not find this book quite so indispensable as I do. I simply cannot get along without it," Vilhjálmur Stefánsson wrote). And he collected Arcticana with intelligence and enthusiasm. He was one of the founders of the National Geographic Society in 1888, remained a trustee for nearly fifty years, till his death. He assembled, organized, and developed the War Department Library; he started many projects in it. He was the first of the founders of the Free Public Library of Washington, too.

In the 1890's he began his study of early American government documents. He was a busy man, with the Arctic business and the Signal Office and a general's duties. And he had never had formal education. But the combination of his scientific work, his government service, and his patriotism drove him to want to put in order all the old things of the government he kept finding in his War Department Library. And elsewhere, too. His study began with the presentation to the American Historical Association in 1896 of a paper, with appended bibliography, *Public Documents of the Early Congresses, 1789–1793* (AHA, *Annual Report*, 1896. Vol. I, 1109-1248). He found scholars so interested that he went on to study the whole period before the beginning of the Serial Set in 1817, and had almost finished his work in 1898 when President McKinley summoned him one day, took him before the cabinet in session, and placed him in complete charge of all telegraphic, electrical, and communications work in the Spanish American War.

With this, General Greely began to modernize, indeed revolutionize communications in the military services. Under his direction between 1898 and 1904, the Army replaced the courier on horseback with electrical devices; under his supervision the Signal Corps built 1,000 miles of telegraph in Porto Rico, 3,800 miles in Cuba, 250 miles in China, 13,500 miles in the Philippines, 3,900 miles in Alaska. That big thick bibliography he had compiled had to be abandoned. He gave it to the press as it was; in 1900 Congress brought it out: *56th Congress, 1st Sess. Senate Document 428. Public Documents of the First Fourteen Congresses 1789–1817.* Later, in the midst of other duties, he published a supplementary list, noting errors in his previous work, adding many titles (AHA, *Annual Report,* 1903. Vol. I, 343-406). And he contemplated his whole work, in spite of its deficiencies, with pride. The *American State Papers* had contained 2,464 documents for this period. He had listed and identified upwards of 5,000.

Greely did not go back to bibliography. He was too busy supporting Langley in the first experiments in power flight, too busy with the earliest work in wireless, with the first imaginings of radio. In 1906 he became Major General. He terminated the Ute Indian rebellion; as commander of the Pacific Division he was in charge of all relief operations after the San Francisco earthquake. In 1908 he retired. And from then till his death (a few months after he received the Congressional

Medal of Honor for his Polar Expedition heroism) he spent his time writing, collecting, speaking, corresponding, principally about the Arctic. He traveled widely through the world, he had friends everywhere among scientists, statesmen, soldiers. For several years he was professor of geography at George Washington University. His tall, stately figure with its luxuriant beard was a fixture in the national capital. Chief Justice Taft was heard to say, "I am glad to see once more the only two permanent things in Washington: the Washington monument, and General Greely." General Billy Mitchell wrote his biography, dedicated it to the youth of America. He was proud, he said, to be one of the hero's disciples. But General Mitchell nowhere mentioned Greely's great bibliography, the work for which chiefly today, in the age of air and the atom when the wild north holds no more a mystery, we remember his various name.

One time Greely wrote in an autograph album of a Philadelphia admirer a sentiment out of that nineteenth century from which he sprang. Bibliographers will perhaps like to imagine that he could have been thinking as well of his work on the early congresses as of his grim years in the frozen white wastelands, when he set down the words, "Heights charm us; the paths which lead to them do not."

Greely did a better job than professional bibliographers, in a field they seemed to touch with reluctance, certainly with a lack of understanding. When Paul Leicester Ford in the 1880's prepared his *Some Materials for a Bibliography of the Official Publications of the Continental Congress, 1774–1789,* published first serially in successive numbers of the *Bulletin of the Boston Public Library,* 1888, then as a book in Brooklyn, he ignored completely the meaning of those words "Official Publications," and included reprints from American and even British presses, which were not official in any sense, and not even Congress issues.

The best opportunity for careful study and listing of all federal issues came in the 1930's, when R. W. G. Vail reached Volume XXVI of his completion of Sabin's *Bibliotheca Americana,* the volume with the heading "United States" in alphabetical order. The entry he made is to historians a serious disappointment: "It was the intention of Joseph Sabin," wrote Dr. Vail, "to enter under 'United States' the titles of documents published by the federal government which he considered to have historical importance. Because of the magnitude of the undertaking it has been decided to omit these titles here, and to refer the student to the following sources of bibliographical information." He then referred the student to the *Journals of the Continental Congress,* Evans, Greely with his more than five thousand titles before 1817, Poore, the 1911 *Checklist,* the 1902 *Annotated Index,* and Mudge's *Guide;* he added the observation that many governmental publications omitted in Greely are to be found in The American Antiquarian Society, Harvard College, The Library of Congress, and The New York Public Library.[7] A listing even of these last items alone would have been a distinct service to historians, but Dr. Vail, I understand, was granted neither the time nor the money and staff to pursue the subject.

Earlier, Joseph Sabin himself had not been very much interested in government documents as books, and the intention he expressed to record the "important" ones cannot have been very serious. In his own part of his great work, he began to list the series of Session Laws under the heading "Congress," but after only a few entries tired of it, saying "It would not be difficult [which I consider far from true], but it would be almost useless [which I regard as an error in judgment], to continue this list of the acts of the different sessions of each successive Congress; let it suffice to remark that they are continuous, and, with the increased number and importance of the states, have become extremely voluminous. . . ." [8] The exact meaning of his remark about "the increased number and importance of the states" escapes me. Of the series of House (Miscellaneous) Documents he listed one only, and dismissed the rest with a confession of defeat: "These 'Documents' are issued at each session of the Congress. . . . They consist of such papers as are printed for the use of the members, and cover many topics of historical importance." [9] Many topics of historical importance—it is the phrase of a bibliographer overwhelmed with his materials. And reports of congressional committees he acknowledged to be "an important series; but they are too voluminous for us to attempt to give their titles." [10]

"Too voluminous, useless, the magnitude of the undertaking"—from the historian's point of view it is too bad. Lacking the definitive exposition Sabin might have given us but did not, we are left with one of the largest, one of the most significant segments of the American written and published record uncatalogued, imperfectly

THE BRADFORDS' FIRST JOURNAL

(Copy in the Collections of Mrs. Joseph Carson)

This pristine copy with large margins, bound in contemporary gilt-tooled calf, is apparently the proof copy of the famous *Journal,* for on page 132 where all other copies have the printed legend, "A True Copy, / Charles Thomson / Secretary," this example has printed the words "A True Copy," followed by Thomson's signature in manuscript. The word "Secretary" does not appear. The printed errata note on page 3, calling attention to the typographical error on page 80, does appear, however, so I assume that Thomson sent these pages back to the Bradfords, signed and approved, and they then set up his signature and the word "Secretary" on page 132. Bound in with the 132-page *Journal* are "To Peyton Randolph, Esq.," p. 133-34, and "To the King's Most Execellent Majesty," p. 135-44, without the separate January, 1755 title page. Among The Library Company of Philadelphia's three copies of this book is one with the separate title page for the *Petition* and the *Gage Letter* bound in. On the reverse of this separate title page the Bradfords printed this legend: "Those who chuse to bind up the following Sheets with the JOURNAL, are desired to destroy this Leaf." Most chose, and the separate title page is very hard to find today.

JOURNAL

OF THE

PROCEEDINGS

OF THE

CONGRESS,

Held at PHILADELPHIA,

September 5, 1774.

PHILADELPHIA:

Printed by WILLIAM and THOMAS BRADFORD,
at the *London Coffee-House.*

M,DCC,LXXIV.

understood, in large part unappreciated and virtually unknown.[11]

Now in these lectures I cannot make this segment known. You would not wish me to read a monograph, or dwell tediously on "points." It is not easy to talk the language of bibliography gracefully. I had first imagined it might be agreeable to dwell affectionately on the "great" documents, describing each element in their composition, each stage in their printing. But others before me have dwelt affectionately in those same precincts; and in the study of government publications the "great" documents are not the story anyway. The government is, for our purposes, an author. Its productions are to be treated as if we were describing an author collection. The story lies in the little things, the book-by-book development of the author's career. In the "great" documents, details would defeat us—details even of exactly how much was printed. There is still a great deal of that to be discovered. When Mr. Michael J. Walsh investigated the first broadside printings of the Declaration of Independence a few years ago, he observed that Paul Leicester Ford in 1888 had listed five editions; I. Minis Hay in 1900, eight; W. C. Ford in 1906, ten; Evans in 1909, eleven; he himself by 1949 had identified nineteen. [12] Unquestionably, for many other official imprints of the forty years, the same enlargement of our knowledge can be expected.

General Greely's five thousand titles, a partial list of government publications from 1789 through 1817, added to the perhaps six hundred publications of the Continental Congress from 1774 to 1789, represent the corpus of literature we are considering. It is not details of each, but the appeal of the whole subject matter, which I must try to exhibit.

For a collector, would it not be a worthy pursuit to seek a copy of the *Association,* that first book ever published by what became the American government? For the political scholar, would it not be suggestive to know that the structural history of our constitution really begins with the first *Rules and Articles for the Better Government of the Troops,* published on June 30, 1775, the first orderly description of powers inhering in a central government? What collector of American law has prized the first case officially reported and published by the national government, or even knows what it was—a case in court martial, publicly recorded, while civilian cases would continue to be privately reported for nearly a century?

Collectors love "firsts," because they are the small beginnings of big things. Superb examples await them in this neglected area of American government documents. And some useful, even some surprising lights fall on our history when public documents are brought together in one view. The bibliographer of the early years of our government will be somewhat startled to discover how much of its evolution, how much of its steady accretion of power was in the military field, how many of the techniques of administration were first developed not from political principle but from the urgent necessities of war. Had historians long ago considered this evident fact of the Revolutionary Congresses, the place of war powers under John Adams and Lincoln, under Wilson and Roosevelt and Truman, under Chase and Taft and

Hughes and Vinson might possibly have caused less trouble in the state.

But historians have not. They and bibliographers have ignored the essential problem of "publication" by the government. To "publish" a law is a sovereign act. Legally, the word *publish* has had a long history. The town crier is part of that history; so is the sheriff nailing a proclamation to an oak tree on a medieval manor; so is the complicated ritual of the sign manual of the British Crown; so is the history of printing and licensing to print.[13] Now the American revolutionists had the British precedents, and they had the routines of thirteen colonial governments behind them. "Publication" as a legal reality was no mystery to them. But it seems to have been a mystery to the Fords, Paul Leicester and Worthington Chauncey, and to Evans and Sabin and most of the others who have listed American books. The Fords were among the first scholars to study the history of government in America bibliographically, but curiously neither brother made the necessary distinction between what the Congress published as an official act, and what private printers reprinted from the official papers as commercial ventures.

This distinction I insist upon. I propose, that a list of the things published by official direction or order shall show, in various ways, the vitality and development of the social organization that made us one and, as we say, made us free. The bibliographical notes W. C. Ford added to his volumes of the *Journals of the Continental Congress* might have done this. They do not.[14] By following his brother's list, and including much that was not official, Ford permitted his notes to cloud and bedim the problem. We must, in truth, hope some day for an analysis of the period he made particularly his own, on principles completely different from those that governed his work.

In history, that which happened takes on a sort of inevitability; in retrospect we conclude it had been bound to happen. From this too-easy view arise our popular myths of history, and our too-simple theories. The historian's task is to free himself of theories. He must think himself back until he is an actor on the stage, looking forward day to day, taking the hard decisions men took with all the uncertainties of life before them.

It was apparent to no one in September, 1774, that the Congress of deputies gathering in the Carpenters' Hall would be the seed from which a government, first federal, then national, would emerge. The delegates came with varying, even conflicting instructions, some from conventions, some from legislatures. None of the instructions said, "go to Philadelphia and form a government." Little was expected, beyond resolutions, petitions, and proposals for better imperial administration. There had, after all, been congresses before—at Albany in '54, New York in '65. Yet a government was just what these delegates did form, a primitive, grass-roots American government, without plan indeed or formal structure but with such actual powers as came from the support and enthusiasms of the aroused elements of the people.

They did so almost accidentally, when they published and signed the *Association,* on October 20, 1774. The

Association was a call to political action, a program of collecting "his majesty's loyal subjects" in North America together in a "non-importation, non-consumption, and non-exportation" pact, erecting committees of enforcement and inspection in every county, city, and town, urging price-fixing against inflation, and calling for further supporting actions by conventions in each colony. At this one stroke, Congress gave shape and unity and a continental focus to the widespread but unorganized congeries of local committees of correspondence on which, before this, the impetus and administration of the revolutionary movement had depended. "The signature of the Association," says the historian Hildreth, "may be considered as the commencement of the American Union."

The *Association* was not the first publication issued by the Congress. It was the second. The first was a quarto broadside of September 22, an "extract from the minutes" printed by the Bradfords, in which the Congress requested merchants and others to suspend all trade with Britain until the delegates had made public their decisions on how best to conduct resistance. The second, which should be considered Item Number One in the publishing history of the American government, was no such request. The twelve-page octavo *Association* was full of firm language and the threat of popular sanctions. A committee of five had prepared the document. Congress "Ordered, That this Association be committed to the press, and one hundred and twenty copies struck off." William and Thomas Bradford printed the one hundred twenty copies on thick paper, nine pages of text, the last three pages blank for the members of

Congress to sign their names. At least two of these copies autographed by the members have survived. One is
in The Historical Society of Pennsylvania. A second
issue contained the names printed instead of autographed, and the text occupies eleven pages. It is not
too much to say of this little book, the authorized official printing of the *Association,* that it is the first act
binding on the American people generally of a consti-
tuted American authority larger than, apart from, the
colonial commonwealths. It is the recorded beginning
of the American government.[15]

Of course, the *Association* was reprinted throughout
the colonies, in newspapers everywhere, in separates by
printers in New Haven and Salem, as well as in volumes
collecting the proceedings of Congress. It was even
rhymed and set to music in a burlesque by the egregious
Rivington of New York. These reprints are not government documents. Reprints measure public acceptance,
popular effect. They are the products of private enterprise seizing on public interest. And public interest,
which Congress designed to reach, still had to be shaped
as it was reached. The delegates to the Congress dared
not share with the public the misgivings and doubts of
their debates. Over their deliberations and proceedings,
the Congress, the Federal Convention, and for many
years the Senate of the new government threw a cloak
of secrecy, a necessary, probably a wholesome part of
the revolutionary process. People were entitled to know
—indeed constantly demanded to know—what the delegates were doing, but for many years all they would receive from the government would be the finished product, the results of debates couched in forms calculated

to elicit support and agreement. Secrecy of debate became a fetish with some, a principle with others, an
issue to everyone. Historians have disapproved of it, because it makes their job of reconstruction so very hard.
But secrecy freed debate; when it was abandoned, congressmen began talking more to constituents than to
colleagues. The present *Congressional Record* with its
fantastic overload of things unsaid but included in the
extended columns of "leave to print" is not the most
intelligent kind of corrective to the suspicion with which
citizens regarded their representatives caballing behind
closed doors. When secrecy was abandoned, too, government could no longer be what John Quincy Adams
thought in a free state it should be, the teacher and
tutor, the improver of a people.[16]

The First Continental Congress had some such impression of its function. Persuasion was its purpose, persuasion of Americans principally, but of Englishmen as
well. Chatham's praise of its state papers is well known:
"My lords, I must declare and avow, that in the master
states of the world, I know not the people or the senate,
who in such a complication of difficult circumstances,
can stand in preference to the delegates of *America,*
assembled in general congress at *Philadelphia.*" The
Congress' work was, for its importance, quickly done,
mostly shaped and finished in the last week, before the
delegates rose on Wednesday, October 26, and there-
upon published with incredible speed. The day after
the *Association* was voted, the *Address to the People of
Great Britain* and the *Memorial to the Inhabitants of
the British American Colonies* were adopted, and the
delegates resolved that they "be immediately committed

to the press; and that no more than one hundred and twenty copies of each be struck off, without further orders from the Congress." The Bradfords published both documents together in one thirty-six page octavo; they were reprinted in Coventry the next year, and the *Address to the People of Great Britain* in London, but so far as I can discover there was no other separate American reprint of the two addresses alone. Three days later, however, October 24, the Bradfords bound up their second (eleven-page) *Association* and their printing of both the *Address* and *Memorial* in a single volume, entitled *Extracts from the Votes and Proceedings of the American Continental Congress* (8vo, 50 pp., numbered 36, thus: tp, v. bl., Association 12 numbered pp., Address and Memorial, 1-36) which bore on its title page the legend, "Published by Order of the Congress." I cannot find that Congress actually did order this edition, and if it did not, then the emission was in violation of the restriction of publication of all three documents to one hundred twenty copies each. That restriction, of course, was never, or almost never, intended really to restrict. All it probably meant was that Congress would *pay* for no more than one hundred twenty copies. The purpose of any publication at all was publicity, and Congress had every reason to be pleased with, indeed to desire, wide general distribution of its papers. Still, the one hundred twenty copies made the official first issue, and apparently we must regard the Bradfords' first *Extracts* as a commercial, not an official adventure. The legend, "published by order of the Congress," soon to become so familiar, in this its very first use seems to have been spurious. But Congress had no reason to object, and the texts were certainly the official, published-by-order texts the Bradfords had used in the first issues.

This first *Extracts* sold out at once, and on October 27 the Bradfords published a second book with the same title—published it in four states with the same date of issue—which they made up from settings they already had or were composing. The four states differ in pagination, containing either 63, 63, 65, or 77 pages, with varying foliation. Let us call these, in hope of clarifying the difficult printing history of this famous landmark of the Revolution, the second, third, fourth, and fifth *Extracts*. They contain the *Association,* the *Address,* and the *Memorial,* as did the first *Extracts,* but they also contain the first printing of the *Declaration of Rights and Grievances,* which Congress had adopted on October 14 but had not previously ordered printed. I say *ordered* printed: the title pages of the four October 27 *Extracts* are all the same, and all contain the same legend as the first *Extracts:* "Published by Order of the Congress." The meaning of this is not sharp and clear. It is, however, perfectly clear that the Bradfords, having produced by now five separate volumes in less than a week, had accustomed their readers to a way of proceeding, and Congress having adjourned, no one was in a position to protest. And it is clear, too, that the printers were determined to assemble all congressional papers together in a single work, which would make a steadily salable book, rather than publish them one by one as broadsides or pamphlets.

Annapolis, Boston, Hartford, New York, Newport, Norwich, Providence, and Williamsburg printers reissued the enlarged *Extracts* as soon as they got hold of a copy of one of the Bradfords' October 27 editions. (The first, October 24, edition, lacking the *Declaration of Rights and Grievances,* seems not to have been reprinted anywhere.) Paul Leicester Ford assigns, incidentally, the premier place among the four states of the October 27 *Extracts* to the one which contains 63 pages, and breaks with these contents: ½t, v. bl.; tp, v. bl.; Resolves 12 pp.; Association 12 pp.; "To the People" 15 pp.; "To the Inhabitants" pp. 16-36. He does not give his reasons, and I cannot imagine any printing practices in the Bradfords' beehive that would make any such assignment of priority possible. Or, indeed, necessary.

Rarely has a print shop been busier than was the Bradfords' establishment at the London Coffee House on Front Street that Thursday, October 27, 1774, the day after Congress adjourned. For that day the intrepid proprietors announced still a third publication, which was the whole of the enlarged *Extracts* from previous settings, with something added: the *Letter to the Inhabitants of Quebec,* drafted by Dickinson, which Congress had adopted on its last day, October 26, and transmitted to the Bradfords just too late for inclusion in the books they had already assembled for distribution. This we must call the sixth *Extracts*. It contains the first official printing of the *Letter to Quebec;* the whole volume with this addition was, like the others that lacked it, reprinted immediately in most of the colonies by enterprising tradesmen. The *Letter to Quebec* alone was reprinted by Dilly and Almon in London, and also in part as a supplement to *Plain Truth,* which Bell printed in Philadelphia in 1776. The Bradfords stitched and wrapped their setting of it as a separate, too, which may easily be identified because it bears the pagination 37-50 in this form.

In Connecticut, the colony itself paid for the reprint of the *Extracts,* issued by Timothy Green of New London on November 3. This is a government document, but a document of the Connecticut government. In this New London imprint, Congress' resolutions answering the Suffolk Resolves and encouraging the hard-beset inhabitants of Massachusetts was printed, its first appearance outside of newspapers. Its second appearance was in Rivington's reprint of the sixth *Extracts* in New York. These, and all the other many local reprints, bear the sentence on their title pages, "Published by Order of the Congress," which is of course not to be taken to mean a congressional authorization of each printing, if it means anything in the way of authorization at all. One 1775 New York edition, by John Holt, says with a certain agreeable accuracy, "Reprinted from copies published by order of the Congress." But in his second printing of this edition, Holt did not bother. Like all the rest, he said simply, "Published by Order of the Congress." None of these reprints is properly a federal government document, none but the Bradfords' imprints, and two more.

For the Congress itself added two official editions of the *Letter to Quebec.* The very name *Quebec* obliged the delegates to think of foreign languages. They ordered the translation of the *Letter* into German and French—German for Pennsylvanians, French for the very *habitants* for whom in part at least the *Letter* was actually intended. Heinrich Miller published a German edition of the whole of the Bradfords' sixth *Extracts,* in a seventy-six page small octavo, which he announced was "Herausgegeben auf Befehl des Congresses"; DuSimitiere translated the *Letter to Quebec* into French, and Fleury Mesplet, newly arrived in Philadelphia, printed two thousand copies for distribution in Canada. These are both official government documents, America's first official publications in foreign tongues.

If the Bradfords were busy, so was Congress as it prepared to adjourn. On October 25, the day before the end, the delegates adopted their *Petition to the King.* Richard Henry Lee had prepared the first draft, John Dickinson had completely rewritten it, and John Adams and Patrick Henry had each taken some hand in the final version. Now Evans lists only one 1774 separate printing of the *Petition,* that by Isaiah Thomas in Boston, which is not of course an official document, but a reprint. Evans has some justification for his omission of the Bradfords' printing, in strictly bibliographical analysis, because the Bradfords were moving so fast by now to keep up with the finish of Congress' work that their first separate of the *Petition* became, in effect, an off-print. Since the *Petition to the King,* along with the *Association,* is the other positive affirmation of political sovereignty the First Congress made as a governing body, there is some reason for considering its printing history realistically.

The New York delegates wrote home, as the *Petition* was adopted, that it would not be printed at once, for "in point of Decorum" it could be given no public view until it had been "laid before the Throne." [17] The

Bradfords felt no such delicacy, and as a matter of fact their *Petition* was already printed and out before the New Yorkers' letter went off. "The printers," observed Caesar Rodney, "are very apt to get the whip-hand of their neighbours . . ." [18]

What the Bradfords did, to meet the urgent public demand for news of the Congress' work, was abruptly to change from the title *Extracts* to a new title, as soon as the whole of Secretary Thomson's minutes had been delivered to them. Apparently, though it seems a physical impossibility, they made their change on that same busy day after Congress' adjournment, October 27, when they issued what is today a book of the greatest rarity, *Journal of the Proceedings of the Congress,* an octavo of 132 pages, not to be confused with the later serial volumes bearing the same title. If we are to believe the Bradfords' dating, it was no less than the sixth book announced as published on that Thursday the 27th by their workmen. And while we need not assume that *all* the work of setup and assembly was done then, certainly it was started that day, and continued at a fierce pace. In the *Pennsylvania Packet* for November 21 is an announcement that the *Journal* will be published "this afternoon." Scholars have sometimes used this as establishing the date of issue to be November 21. But already one delegate had written back on October 31 that Congress' proceedings "are now in the press, part of which is published." [19] And another sent the *Journal* home as early as November 7. [20]

Someone has called this first volume to bear the title *Journal* the "original" edition. There is very little point in that, for it was neither the first of Congress' publications, nor the first of the serial set of later journals. It might better be thought of as a seventh edition of the *Extracts,* expanded. But it contained so much new material, so much new setting of previously printed stuff, that we may believe the Bradfords received Thomson's minutes as the full record they had been waiting for and building toward, the climax of their astonishingly busy week. Proof that they had been waiting and preparing is the fact that they had a cut all ready. Someone had been commissioned to design it, and someone in that bustling shop had found time to manufacture it, a primitive insignium of an American sovereignty. The title page of this first *Journal* bears an emblematical device, twelve hands representing the twelve colonies in Congress, supporting a column crowned with a liberty cap, the base founded firmly on Magna Charta. The motto is *Hanc Tuemur Hac Nitimur,* which may be freely rendered, "We behold Liberty, we strive for Her."

And now, just as this first *Journal* came off the press, too late for inclusion in it, the Bradfords received two more documents from Secretary Thomson. They bore no substantive relationship to each other, no relationship except this accident of arriving at the same tardy time. The first was the letter of General Gage from Boston to Peyton Randolph, President of the Congress, written in answer to Congress' letter to him; the second was the *Petition to the King.*

Promptly, the Bradfords set these in type, numbering the pages as 133-144 of the *Journal,* with an unfoliated title page preceding. The whole publication with these added pages may be called the second issue of the

Journal. Those customers who had already bought the first *Journal* could buy the *Petition* and the *Gage Letter* as an eight-page separate without title page. These examples commence with the words, "To Peyton Randolph, Esq.," the beginning of Gage's letter, and the first page number is 133. When they found time, of course, the Bradfords put a separate title page to the little off-print, and though they changed neither the typesetting nor the pagination, their added title page began, *The Petition of the Continental Congress to the King. And General Gage's Letter.* But they did not find time to do this for several months, and the date on their separate title page is the next year, 1775. Neither Evans nor Hildeburn lists it, though P. L. Ford had done so in 1888, and W. C. Ford did so in 1906. I have seen the copy owned by William Logan Fox, Esq., at Broad Axe, Pa. These two separates are the same printing, and it is proper to consider all three as one.

And with this second issue of the *Journal,* the Bradfords' hectic striving to give Congress' work at once to the public came to a grateful end.[21] "Yesterday the Congress broke up," John Dickinson wrote to Arthur Lee on October 27.[22] "You will immediately know their Proceedings from publications." And immediately, the whole world did. Ten publications had been issued, the first ten documents of the first body that can be called an American government, in this short period in the fall of 1774. They are as follows:

1. Broadside to the Merchants
2. Association (1)
   2,a. Association (2)

3. Address to Great Britain and Memorial to the Inhabitants of the Colonies
4. Extracts (1)
5. Extracts (2), with Declaration of Rights and Grievances
   5,a. Extracts (3)
   5,b. Extracts (4)
   5,c. Extracts (5)
6. Extracts (6), with Letter to Quebec
   6,a. Separate, Letter to Quebec
7. Journal (1)
8. Journal (2), with Petition to King and Gage Letter
   8,a. Petition to King, separate with title page
   8,b. Petition to King, separate with title page, dated 1775
9. Extracts, German edition
10. Lettre aux . . . Quebec, French edition

Through the Bradfords' remarkable efficiency and speed, they had entered at once into the stream of general opinion through the available instruments of culture.

These available instruments, incidentally, included newspapers, and since during the next fifteen years the Continental Congress, as it altered from a protesting to an administrating body, regularly released its proceedings to the weekly and daily journals, official publications of the government often appeared first in this fugitive form. Newspaper publications were usually authorized but not ordered by Congress, and of course were not paid for. They are not part of the permanent governmental record we are concerned with. But they were part of the printers' enterprise, and it was from newspaper printings that many of the privately printed separate reissues were drawn.

AITKEN'S MANUSCRIPT ACCOUNT BOOK
(In The Library Company of Philadelphia)

On one double page during the summer of 1776, Aitken noted some printing he did for "Congress Navy board," and various sales of books and paper to individual members as well. The five members he listed here were all Signers of the Declaration: Dr. Rush of Pennsylvania bought blue paper from him; President Witherspoon of New Jersey a blank book ledger; Hooper of North Carolina, Stone of Maryland, Walton of Georgia, all three ordered large quantities of Congress' pamphlet on salt peter (1,800 copies in all), and military tracts and manuals as well. "James Bennet Virg^a Rider," who purchased Simms' *Military Guide,* was probably the express rider Elija Bennett, whom Washington and Congress employed on fast errands.

Friday 30 Aug.t 1776

250 John Morris Esq.r D.r for Convocation
To r Rev Foolscap — 45/ — 1 2 6

Mr Hooper of Congress D.r
paid To 1000 Extracts on Salt a 15/— } 15 —
30/p cent printed
14 for 12 Field Engineer a 22/6 13 10 —

Tuesday 4 —
237 Philad.a Library Comp.y D.r
To 2 Field Engineer 22/6 2 5 —
To 2 Militʸ Discipline 10/— 1 — —
3 5 —

Frid. 6 —
210 C.l James Cochran . 10 —

266 Dr Benj.n Rush D.r
To 1 Rev blue paper . 18 —

203 John Willis D.r to Cash 2 5 —

Pack'd this day & sent Invoice
for rem.dr Boy to be directed Care of Geo.
of this boy Gordon Charlestown for M.r
sentown Roth Wills Bookseller D.r
of Aug 327 12 Vols Penn.a Mag for 1775 a 3 7 19 6
6 Ditto do to bound 12/3 3/3 3 13 6
6 Militʸ Discipline bound 7/6 2 5 —
6 D.o in blue boards 6/ 1 16 —
15 for 12 Petite Guerre 7/6 4 10 —
14 for 12 Field Engineer 22/6 13 10 —
4 Setts Militʸ Gliden 2 Vols 18/3 3 13 —
4 Militʸ Exercise 3/6 . 14 —
24 Lewhi Grammar g.r 12/ 1 4 —
12 Modern Riding Master a 10/ } . 10 —
Carr.d to p. 347 £ 39 14 6

254 Tho.s Store Esq.r of Congress D.r
To 300 Extracts on Salt a 30/ 4 10 —

Geo. Walton Esq.r of Congress D.r
paid To 500 Extracts on Salt — 30/ 7 10 —
100

Tuesd. 10
262 James Hannet Vir.a Rider D.r
To 1 Simmons Militʸ Guide — 1 2 6

254 Geo. Walton Esq.r of Congress D.r
To 1 Petter Musculus . 10 —
To Batchelor of Salamanca 2 D.r . 12 —
By Cash . 5 6

Tuesday 10 Sept.r 1776

246 John Gibson Esq.r D.r
To Art of Speaking . 6 —
To Chesterfields Letters . 10 —
To Terence Delphini . 12 —
To Baxters Horace . 12 —
To Delap's Greek Grammar . 3 —
2 3 —

247 Major Lewis Nicola D.r
To Binding 100 Militʸ Exer. 6 7 10 —

Tuesd. 17
254 Walton Esq.r of Congress D.r
To 1 Field Engineer . 1 2 6
To 1 Militʸ Guide 2 Vols . 1 2 6
To do instruct.n for Officers . 7 6
To 1 do Discipline . 10 —
To 1 Do Exercise . 4 6
3 6 6

202 Mr James Lishman D.r
To 6 q.r Foolscap — 2/3 . 13 6
To Cash . 2 3

Wed. 18
258 Congress D.r
To printing a broad sheet being 500 } 3 15 —
articles for Vessels of war, & paper

191 Benj.n Towne Esq part. D.r
To Cash 6 15 —

170 Benj.n Towne D.r
To ins hist of Man . 10 —
To Essay on Char. of Women . 5 —
Violets Rev. on Education 1 1 —

Frid. 20 —
184 Dr Witherspoon D.r
To 5 quire foolscap ledger 1 5 —

3 Mr Rob.t Patten P.A Atty D.r
To pencil . . 4

Sat. 21
254 Geo Walton Esq.r of Congress D.r
To Sterne's Works 4 Vol . 10 —
To 1 g.s 4.to post . 2 —
To 1 Duodecimo a Novel . 5 —
1 17 —

Tuesd. 24
238 In. Searle Esq.r D.r
To Field Engineer . 1 2 6
To Military Exercise . 4 —

Now the original necessities which first called a Congress into being were in a few months, certainly by May 1775 when the Second Congress met, entirely superseded. More urgent requirements, especially the war already actually in progress, obliged the delegates at once when they resumed work to become, in addition to a deliberative, an administrative body, which is to say, a functioning government. The Association had proved in its first weeks too thin and limited a structure to keep pace with the rapidly increasing tensions of the winter; by the summer of 1775 it was actually a hindrance, for the Congress perforce had to secure the importation of war supplies from abroad. One of the first official publications of 1775 was a broadside relaxing the Association, partially suspending nonimportation, permitting, indeed encouraging, merchants to exchange goods for arms. Congress wanted this resolution known abroad, but it had as yet no secretariat, no machinery for communicating with foreign governments, nor indeed with anyone. The members committed the broadside to the Pennsylvania delegates, whom they "desired to request the Committee of [Correspondence of] this City to forward the same in handbills to the West Indies."

Even before this, a military committee had been appointed. Their report was the Bradfords' publication on June 30, 1775, of the sixteen-page octavo *Rules and Articles for the better Government of the Troops . . . of the Twelve United English Colonies of North America.* This little book was reprinted in New York, Watertown, and Boston; Congress had it translated into French (at a cost of fifteen and a half dollars) and sent a thousand copies of Mesplet's edition along with the troops into Canada. In November a second revised edition was ordered, in which the Bradfords on the title page substituted "Thirteen" for "Twelve" as the number of colonies, now completed. In November, too, the navy committee was ready with its regulations. John Adams had drawn them up; he made the presentation to Congress. The members debated for a day, then approved the regulations and ordered them printed (November 30). The title the Bradfords used was Adams' own heady prose: *Rules for the Regulation of the Navy of the United Colonies of North America; Established for Preserving their Rights and Defending their Liberties, and for Encouraging all those who Feel for their Country, to enter into its Service in that way in which they can be most useful.* Modest as they are, these two *Rules* represent the beginning of the American military manual, and of the continuous history of our national military law. More than that, they are the beginning of an administrative activity originating at the top of a governmental structure. In them, Congress described its powers, and placed itself at the head of a war machine, with everything that involved.

It involved a good deal. With no administrative machinery, a new government was arising in the world, arising because of the activity-creating needs to appoint officers, pay troops, outfit ships, issue letters of marque, publish and confirm orders, assert a political supremacy over military actions, and most pressing of all, procure powder and shot. Congress published a twelve-page pamphlet, *Several Methods of Making Salt Peter,* from a manuscript one well-meaning patriot sent in; it published the articles of capitulation of Montreal; it printed publicly the intercepted letters, a thousand copies "to go with the dispatches" so the troops in Canada and Massachusetts would be informed. And in this year, 1775, it took over the running of the Post Office.

This last we must notice. For carrying the mails was, of all the essential governmental services on the continent, the first one to be domesticated and nationalized. Franklin, home from England and a delegate in Congress, was appointed Post Master General on July 26, with power to select deputies. Like the appointment of Washington to the Army, this was an act of government emerging from no constitution or charter, but required by the exigencies of the moment. Franklin himself added somewhat to the color of sovereignty in Congress' acts by requesting the New Jersey delegates to nominate deputy postmasters throughout their state, which the delegates promptly did. Two broadsides printed by Dunlap for the Congress in this year, one giving tables of rates, the other telling postmasters how to keep their accounts, are more than philatelic items: they deserve to be noticed as the first publications in the civilian administrative history of the nation. In the same category, we may observe, is the Bradfords' broadside list of the names of the delegates in Congress, the one-celled ancestor of the later elaborate biographical directories of members of Congress and roster lists.

Busy as it is with these matters, the Second Continental Congress still remains in 1775 a forum for policy and persuasion. Dickinson, over the strenuous and bitter objections of the brace of Adamses, succeeds in carrying through the Olive Branch Petition; the important bibliographical observation to be made about it is that Congress never bothered to order it published. There is no official edition of this Second Petition to the King, apart from the *Journal,* and only one American printing, that one made by certain timid New Yorkers of tory inclinations.

On the other hand, the *Declaration of the Causes and Necessity of Taking Up Arms,* printed by the Bradfords (apparently without special orders from Congress), was reprinted in newspapers at once, and as a separate in New York (twice), in Newport, Providence, Watertown, Portsmouth, Bristol, and London. One place it seems not to have been published, or at least not printed, was the one place where Congress ordered it to be, by General Washington on his arrival at the camp before Boston. So it is curiously doubtful if there is in the proper sense a government imprint of this deeply moving, important document. The *Declaration of the Causes* was sensible and mild; the confusion that once existed over its authorship, be it noted, has been finally and surely settled by Mr. Julian Boyd.[23] A second *Letter to Quebec* was issued, in French and English; a second *Address to the Inhabitants of Great Britain,* an *Address to the People of Ireland.* Jefferson drafted, Congress printed the American answer to Lord North's proposals of conciliation; Congress printed, also, an answer to the king's Proclamation of Rebellion.

Policy, persuasion, administration—by the end of 1775 the pattern is fixed. And the greatest of these, for the future of government in America, is administration. In little ways and big, Congress has become spokesman and administrator, the focus of a continent-wide activity.

The climactic end of this formative stage comes in the spring of 1776, with three acts of sovereignty at international law. Dunlap printed them: two broadside resolutions concerning privateers, March 23 and April 3; instructions to commanders of American vessels April 3 (Congress is now issuing letters of marque and reprisal, an act of nationhood); and the resolution of May 10, published May 15, directing the colonies to form state governments. Independence is at hand. After a year and a half of developing experience, Congress is a governmental organization ready for it.

The major bibliographical event of 1776—indeed, it would become us to refer to it with pride, as the major bibliographical event in American printing history— was, of course, the issuing on July 5 of the broadside Declaration of Independence. I say July 5 with some hope and some confidence of being right, though the point is in dispute. Jefferson, several weeks, or it may have been months, or it may have been years later,[24] wrote this note, which has given much trouble: "the debates [on the Declaration] having taken up the greater parts of the 2d. 3d. & 4th days of July were, in the evening of the last closed. the declaration was reported by the commee., agreed to by the house, and signed by every member present except Mr. Dickinson." [25] Now if Jefferson meant, as some have assumed he did, that all three events—report, agreement, and signing—took place on the fourth, then there was a scene of signing which has been lost to history. It is not entirely unimaginable, though the thought takes us far beyond the existing records. Certainly the Committee of the Whole

did finish its debate, rise, and report on the fourth—
Jefferson says in the evening, and we have every reason
to think he was right in this, for Congress had been
sitting each day for a week past into the darkening twi-
light hours. It was their recent habit. But not *too* late
on the fourth, we believe, for *after* Congress adjourned
Caesar Rodney still had time to write his famous letter
to his brother before he retired: [26]

I arrived in Congress (tho detained by Thunder and Rain)
time Enough to give my Voice in the matter of Independence.... We have now Got through with the Whole of the
declaration and Ordered it to be printed, so that you will
soon have the pleasure of seeing it—Hand-bills of it will be
printed and sent to the Armies, Cities, County Towns &ᶜ.
To be published or rather proclaimed in form. ...

Still, evening it undoubtedly was before the committee
rose. And you will notice that Rodney, in that wonderful letter of his which was once one of Dr. Rosenbach's
treasures, writes on the evening of the fourth that hand-
bills *will be* printed. They are not there in Congress
yet.

Certainly Congress did right away that same evening
receive and adopt the Committee of the Whole report,
and order the printing. The official action reads thus:
"Ordered That the declaration be authenticated and
printed. That the committee appointed to prepare the
declaration superintend and correct the press. That copies of the declaration be sent to the several assemblies,
conventions & committees or councils of safety and to
the several commanding officers of the continental
troops that it be proclaimed in each of the united states
& at the head of the army." [27] The requirement that

the committee "superintend the press" is unique in our annals. It explains what Jefferson, Adams, Franklin, Sherman, and Livingston did after Congress adjourned that evening: they went to Dunlap's printing house.

And now, if after the official order to print and before adjournment, there was a signing on the evening of the fourth, as Jefferson seems to say there was, the plain question is, what document exactly could it have been to which the delegates put their names? Certainly not the broadside copy. The members did not sit around and wait through that whole rainy night while Dunlap took the manuscript, set it in type, impressed his sheets, and delivered the handbills. Speculatively, to make the most of Jefferson's remark, since the most has been made of it, there are two possibilities, both of them admittedly wild.

The first is that Congress may have had secretly printed, for the use of its members only, the Report of the Committee of Five (June 28) submitting the Declaration to the house. This was the text being debated, and the members certainly had to have some copy to read while they debated. If such a printing occurred, it may be that one copy, with manuscript corrections entered after the three days' debate, was signed. But this would be a printing of which no public record was made anywhere by anybody, and of which no copy nor any reference to any copy has survived. It is completely unlikely that any such preprinting occurred. Equally secret and confidential was the draft of the Articles of Confederation, considered this same month. Congress did have Dunlap make a printing of it, with this strict injunction: [28]

Resolved, that 80 copies, and no more, of the confederation, as brought in by the committee, be immediately printed, and deposited with the secretary, who shall deliver a copy to each member:

That the printer be under oath to deliver all the copies which he shall print, together with the copy sheet, to the secretary, and not to disclose either directly or indirectly, the contents of the said confederacy:

That no member furnish any person with his copy, or take any steps by which the said confederation may be reprinted, and that the secretary be under the like injunction.

This astonishing secret order survived on Thomson's minutes. It is not really to be thought that a similar house imprint of the Declaration could have existed, without at least this much of a minute on the journal. Nor is it thinkable that a copy, once signed by the members, should have been lost or mislaid.

Secondly, it is within the realm of speculative possibility that the delegates may have signed their names at the end of that long day's discussion to the manuscript itself of the Report of the Committee of Five, after it had been corrected. This we shall never know, for though almost every other document of these three weeks has survived, even rough notes and drafts, this crucial manuscript of the Committee of Five, the text as debated, has, oddly enough, disappeared.[29] Perhaps it disappeared in Dunlap's print shop. He had to have some copy to give his printers; this was the likely copy for Jefferson, Franklin, Livingston, Adams, and Sherman, any one or all of them, to take to him.

Now both of these speculations are so far beyond

reasonable acceptance that we ought to conclude no
signing at all on the fourth took place, in spite of Jefferson's sentence. Hazelton thinks this; so did Burnett;
so, if you will excuse my saying so, do I. So does Mr.
Boyd, for nine good reasons which he enumerates in
irresistible series.[30] Yet Mr. Boyd knows the wonders of
archival studies as perhaps no one else, and he sensibly
urges this warning, that all the evidence against a signing on the fourth is negative evidence. "No member of
Congress ever stated in so many words," he writes, "that
a Declaration was *not* signed on 4 July." No member
but Thomas McKean, that is, who in 1796 and again
in 1813 stated so many things, some of them known to
be erroneous, that his faulty memory disturbs rather
than clarifies the problem. I think Mr. Boyd is entirely
right to observe that there remains a question raised by
Jefferson's statement that is not yet fully closed.[31] The
author of the Declaration was never careless when he
wrote of that summer's transactions; neither is the editor of Jefferson's *Papers* when he assembles his data.

Historians and bibliographers admittedly give themselves concern over what may seem to busy people matters very minor indeed. But there is a substantial question here in this matter of a signing on the fourth. The
Declaration of Independence, you will recall, ends with
a final clear and precise statement of sovereignty:

That these United Colonies are, and of Right ought to be
FREE AND INDEPENDENT STATES . . . and that as FREE AND
INDEPENDENT STATES, they have full Power to levy War, conclude Peace, contract Alliances, establish Commerce, and do
all other Acts and Things which INDEPENDENT STATES may
of right do.

Congress had already been doing many of those "Acts and Things." But plainly, the delegates regarded their present bold enterprise with the wholesome awe and respect which it did indeed deserve, for to this concluding statement of sovereignty they added a final arresting provision. It is the only time in Anglo-American legislative history that members of a senate enacting an ordinance have required of themselves a testimony of personal responsibility:

And for the support of this Declaration, with a firm Reliance on the Protection of divine Providence, we mutually pledge to each other our Lives, our Fortunes, and our sacred Honor.

The grammatical referent of the pronouns *we* and *each other* is the phrase, "the Representatives of the UNITED STATES OF AMERICA, in GENERAL CONGRESS, Assembled." And that last ringing sentence brings the issue of a signing into the immediate foreground. Was it a necessary part of the enactment, the execution, the validation of the charter, that the highly personal mutual pledge be attested by signature? True enough, the order of the fourth had not required signing, in so many words. It required only authentication, printing, distribution, and proclaiming. But a later order, of July 19, did require that the Declaration "be fairly engrossed on parchment . . . and . . . signed by the members." It is as easy to interpret this as meaning that a previous document had been signed as that one had not.

But again the question is, what document could it have been? Well, there is a third speculative possibility, which would fit all the facts, and offers agreeable mirages to bibliophiles and collectors. Dunlap, we assume, did his work overnight, delivered the broadsides on the fifth. We know he delivered at least some of them then, for Hancock that day sent a copy to the New Jersey Convention, "in obedience to the commands of Congress." [32] (The letters of William Whipple on the 8th and John Adams on the 9th describing "publication" on the 8th refer, not to printing, but to the "publishing and proclaiming" of the Declaration before a great throng of people in the State House Yard by the Pennsylvania Committee of Safety.) [33]

And when Dunlap's broadsides arrived on the morning of the fifth, it is barely possible that the delegates present trooped up to the president's desk and set their hands to a printed copy, while the ink was still wet. Barely possible. Mr. Jefferson could telescope two days together in a sentence, just as any of us do. He could have meant, in his famous remark, that the Declaration was reported by the Committee and agreed to by the Congress on the fourth, and signed by every member present except Mr. Dickinson on the fifth. Mr. Dickinson was not present on the fifth, but then he had not been present on the fourth either, which raises still more questions about Jefferson's remark.

But if it happened so, what became of the signed broadside? It would, one imagines, have been cherished and preserved. It was not. Fourteen copies of the Dunlap broadside are known; none of them bears any manuscript signatures. And this negative evidence, this absence of the most important paper that would ever have passed through Charles Thomson's hands, is enough, in all reason, to confound our third speculation. Unless something else turns up, the mythical signing in July, alas! will go whistling down the wind, and we shall be left with reality.

But something may turn up. Fourteen copies are not enough of this large printing to have survived.[34] So wide was its distribution, so generally was it dispersed through the states that, in spite of the extensive researches of Hazelton, it is not impossible that one day another copy will be found and recognized, not impossible even that one may appear with signatures.

I hope one does. This is the first official version of the Declaration of Independence in any form, this unlovely broadside. The signed manuscript copy on vellum, now reposing in its atom-proof shrine at the National Archives, was not even ordered by Congress to be engrossed till July 19; it was not signed by the members until August 2, and then only by some—others added their signatures in later years. Three and a half weeks before the vellum copy even existed, the Dunlap publication had been officially distributed by President Hancock, and had been wafered into the proper place in his journals by Secretary Thomson. That inserted broadside is still there in the Congress journals where Thomson pasted it, on the morning of July 5, 1776.

It has a strong bibliographical claim to lie in that imposing Archives shrine, along with the engrossed vellum copy, that the people may know the official document which made us, what we had already become in fact, in name a nation.

2

E Pluribus Unum

THE FAMILIAR LAWYERS' MAXIM, *de minimis non curat lex*—the law does not bother itself with little things— is one which could never, not even in the heartiest academic enthusiasms of our day when scholarship is endowed or subsidized and is not obliged to compete in the market place of ideas for attention, be applied to bibliography by its devotees. For bibliography is essentially a science of the little, dealing with tiny data and miniscule observations. Temperamentally, the bibliographer must be an antiquarian.

It borders on the trivial for us to choose, of all the great issues surrounding the new government's beginning in 1789, the problems of printing and publishing. They were the least of controversy, the most routine of matters facing men busy with the high calamities of state. Yet they were essential matters. Without publishing, the government could not proceed, nor could it record what it had done. And if our minikins and molecules of bibliography shed only oblique lights on big affairs, still it is worth remarking that the event they briefly illuminate is the building of a nation.

That nation was new-modeled in structure and spirit

by the Federal Convention of 1787. Its philosophy had been refined and beaten into shape by the year of popular debate over Ratification, 1788. The books of the Ratification Controversy are not part of *official* history. They belong with all their sprightly excitements to another study. But the Constitutional Convention of '87, because it was authorized by Congress, was a governmental body, and its brief publication history deserves at least a glance here.

Brief it was, but still its details are not entirely clear, for bibliographers have neglected this subject, too.[1] In all his four volumes, Dr. Max Farrand nowhere took the trouble to collate known copies of Convention printings. His great work is the weaker therefor. He saw little occasion for doing so, because to every historian of the Convention the problem that looms largest is the profusion of manuscripts he must puzzle over. From late May all through June and July, the delegates at Philadelphia discussed the Virginia and New Jersey plans, which they had in manuscript copies only. The first thing they printed—printed, not published; it was for the members' use only—was the Report of the Committee of Detail, August 6. This they debated for another month; then they made a second printing, also for the use of the delegates only, of the Report of the Committee of Style, which was ordered September 12, but as is plain from McHenry's notes, was given to the printer that day, set up and impressed overnight, and "received, read, and compared" as the first order of business on September 13. Dr. Farrand and many others have called this issue the September 12th printing. In strictest accuracy it should be called September 13th, for that was the day it came from the press. The error, however, is pretty firmly entrenched in our literature and probably will not be changed now.

Dr. Farrand notes, in his general introduction, that "several copies" of these two Convention printings exist, with emendations and marginalia by the various delegates who owned them. But he adds, "these documents are hardly worthy of being reprinted," for the marginalia add nothing not contained in other records.[2] In general he is of course right; there would be no point in extending his volumes by repetitious reprintings of the same document. But had he collated the several copies, he could have made at least one discovery that was, the same year he published the revised and enlarged second edition of his life's work, made by another. During 1937, when Mr. Julian Boyd was preparing a notable exhibition of the Constitution for the celebration of the 150th anniversary of the Convention, he got out of the vaults of The Historical Society of Pennsylvania one of the several known copies of the August 6th printing. It had lain in those vaults since the year 1881: a document of seven numbered leaves, an eighth blank, with an endorsement in an unknown hand, reading "Rough Dr[t] fed[r] Constitution." Throughout were manuscript corrections by Edmund Randolph. Now Farrand, Ford, many bibliographers, many librarians had seen it, but all of them had assumed it was just one of the several known examples of the August 6th printing of the Committee of Detail. Mr. Boyd did what no one else had bothered to do. He studied the document. And he found no less than twelve textual differences between it and the August

6th printing. His was the agreeable experience of identifying the only known copy of the first state of the first issue of our Constitution. The seven numbered leaves were plainly proof sheets, furnished by Dunlap and Claypoole to the Committee of Detail and, from the manuscript revisions inserted by Randolph, it may be assumed the August 6th printing was made.[3]

Sixty copies of this latter were issued, printed on one side only of seven leaves, for the use of the members. Eight of the sixty are now known to exist: among them, those belonging to Brearley, Madison, Johnson, Mason, Gerry, Butler, and Pinckney. The William Samuel Johnson copy in The Library of Congress has manuscript notes in the hand of William Jackson, Secretary to the Convention, made from August 6 through September 3. Presumably, it is the copy Jackson kept on his desk, recording the changes made by the members, and thus deserves to be called the "official" copy. It is possible other copies may turn up, as more papers of the members are brought into public view. The September 13th printing, the Report of the Committee of Style, also for the use of the members only, on one side of four leaves, may likewise appear in new examples in the future: John Dickinson's copy came only a few years ago into The Library Company of Philadelphia.

What Evans calls "the first issue of the Constitution as agreed" he describes as a Dunlap and Claypoole printing in two columns on four pages folio. This printing included the letter of September 17 signed by General Washington as President of the Convention, transmitting the Constitution to Congress; but it also included the resolution of Congress of September 28, submitting

the Constitution to the states for ratification. The printers could not have issued this, at least in its final form,
before September 28, when Congress passed its resolution and Charles Thomson wrote his letter to accom-
pany the Constitution to the various states. I don't know
why Evans should have called this the "first" issue.
There were several printings in the ten days before it
could have appeared. And plainly, it was a Congress,
not a Convention printing. Its particular distinction is
that it was the official text of the new frame of government as accepted by Congress and transmitted by Congress to the states for ratification. Do not dismiss Evans'
error lightly; it was the Constitution of the United
States he was dealing with.

This September 28 printing, incidentally, was actually printed, not by Dunlap and Claypoole in Philadelphia but by John M'Lean at his print shop at No. 41
Hanover Square, in New York, where the Congress was
sitting. Mr. Roscoe C. Hill discovered this when he
edited Volume XXXIII of the *Journals of the Continental Congress* (after W. C. Ford's death, and Gaillard
Hunt's). But as Mr. Hill explains,[4] Dunlap's bills in the
Congress' "Register of Accounts" which still exists in
the Continental Congress Papers in the Library of Congress show the Philadelphia printer charging Congress
£3-10 for one hundred copies of M'Lean's imprint of
September 28; on October 3 he charged £1-4 for another hundred copies (which proves, incidentally, that
there were two states of this issue). Plainly, Dunlap
acted as procurer of the printing in this case. He did
so in other cases, too. Bibliographers ought to note this
official Congress printing of the Constitution of Sep-

tember 28 as "[New York: Printed by John M'Lean, for John Dunlap of Philadelphia, by order of the Congress. 1787]."

The actual "first issue of the Constitution as agreed" was clearly a Convention issue in Philadelphia: Dunlap and Claypoole's large-type, single-column printing in six folio pages beginning "We the People," containing the names (printed) of George Washington, president and deputy from Virginia, and thirty-nine representatives; the resolution of the Convention on its last day, September 17, providing for ratification by the states, signed by Washington, president, and William Jackson, secretary; and the letter of Washington of September 17 transmitting the Constitution to the president of Congress, "By unanimous order of the Convention." This is the printing the Convention ordered in 500 copies— where have they all got to?—and an obvious reason for thinking it the first and officially ordered one is that Dunlap and Claypoole used this typesetting for the four-page supplement of their daily *Pennsylvania Packet* on September 19, which fixes that date, and permits the earlier date of Monday the 17th as the time of this first issue.

Apparently, the Convention never paid Dunlap and Claypoole for it. At least, no bills survived that Dr. Farrand could find. There is a bill for "stationery purchased for the use of the Federal Convention," $36.00; and there is the notation, "to the Clerks employed to transcribe and engross," $30.00, but there is no printer's account. Perhaps Dunlap and Claypoole issued the five hundred copies ordered on a speculation. It would have been a sound risk, so high was the public interest.

The bill for engrossing brings us to the parchment manuscript copy. The first printed issue of the Constitution has not the same official status as we found the first broadside of the Declaration had. In this case, it is quite right that the engrossed manuscript copy should lie in that atom-proof shrine at the National Archives. For the Convention itself ordered the engrossing of the Constitution, when it adjourned about six in the evening on Saturday, September 15. William Jackson's journal, curiously, omits the order. Jackson recorded only this last observation in the *Ayes and Noes:* "The Constitution unanimously agreed to." But McHenry's notes contain the sentence, "Ordered to be engrossed and 500 copies struck." And our best information for that Saturday comes, for once, from that usually inexpressive, unhelpful diarist, George Washington. Washington wrote, late on Saturday the 15th,[5]

concluded the business of Convention, all to signing the proceedings; to effect which the House sat till 6 o'clock; and adjourned 'till Monday that the Constitution which it was proposed to offer to the People might be engrossed— and a number of printed copies struck off.

The clerks worked at their engrossing over Sunday. So did Dunlap and Claypoole's printers at their type forms. Both the engrossed copy and the printed issue were probably ready Monday morning, September 17, when the Convention met for its last day. "Read the engrossed constitution," McHenry's notes begin. And on that day Madison's notes record, "The members then proceeded to sign the instrument." Obviously, it was the engrossed parchment manuscript the Convention was executing as the official Constitution. The hurried engrossers had made errors, and after the fashion of good clerks they noted their errors at the end, before the members signed. You can still see their corrections following Article VII on the faded parchment in the Archives shrine.

The Convention then passed their resolution providing for ratification, and heard the reading of Washington's official letter of transmittal to Congress. These had both been prepared earlier; they had already been set up in type by Dunlap and Claypoole at the end of their six-page printing. Thus the printed issue, ordered at the same time as the engrossed copy, was not the executed Constitution. It was, however, the first public issue, and it was the copy Washington sent to Lafayette on Tuesday, September 18—the day *before* the extra issue of the *Pennsylvania Packet,* you will note; a fact which almost conclusively proves the date of the 17th for the first printing: [6]

My dear Marqs [Washington wrote]: In the midst of hurry, and in the moment of my departure from this City, I address this letter to you. The principal, indeed the only design of it, is to fulfil the promise I made, that I would send to you the proceedings of the Fœderal convention, as soon as the business was closed. More than this, circumstanced as I am at present, it is not in my power to do. nor am I inclined to attempt it, as the enclosure, must speak for itself, and will occupy your thoughts for some time.

It is the production of four months deliberation. It is now a Child of fortune, to be fostered by some and buffeted by others. what will be the General opinion on, or the reception of it, is not for me to decide, nor shall I say any thing for or against it: if it be good I suppose it will work its way good; if bad, it will recoil on the Framers. . . .

Following September 18, of course, printers everywhere published the new frame of government. For the Convention's work, once submitted to Congress in the official copy, was fair game for the people's presses.

Now the new Congress and new executive officers who assembled together in L'Enfant's newly furbished Federal Hall in New York in April, 1789, had to bring the Convention's blueprint into new being, and try, in Washington's colorful but not quite accurate nautical phrase, to work their way good. For guides to printing practices their new government could follow, the Federalists had the publication experience of fifteen years of the Old Congress, and in general that congressional experience is what they did follow. A separate executive, a separate judiciary were new elements in government in 1789. The habit of that old legend, "Printed by Order of the Congress," proved to be an administrative routine too strong to break. By the arrangements prescribed in the new Constitution, Congress furnished the money; it was logical that, where the new departments could manage to avoid the responsibility, Congress should also spend the money. Some day, each department would have a budget so large that it could make its own contracts with printers, but at the outset, and for many years after 1789, indeed to the end of our period, the documents published by the United States were, whatever their departmental origins, ordered printed and paid for by one of the two houses as congressional documents.

Most of them, that is. There are a few exceptions. There were exceptions even during the fifteen years of the Old Congress. Now I do not propose to discuss the issues of those previous fifteen years, 1774–1789, in detail, but I do wish to look at them briefly, as precedents, much as the men who made the new government in 1789 must have looked at them.

One unsatisfactory thing, of course, about the Old Congress in every respect was that it was considered to have failed. As with the Association, when the original necessities which first called the Congress into being were supplanted by more urgent public requirements, which the Congress could not serve, the governmental institution itself had to alter. The failure in vitality shows in the printing record year by year, as we list the number of things the Old Congress ordered published during each of its annual sessions. Counting major identified documents only, the numbers look something like this:

1776	56	1783	24
1777	50	1784	22
1778	39	1785	55
1779	83	1786	47
1780	33	1787	30, & 4 Convention items
1781	12	1788	18
1782	20	1789	2

There was, you will notice, a distinct revival in the year 1779, but in general the Old Congress cannot be said to have burdened the people overmuch with official words. It is not a very large amount of publication for a government which established itself, established the nation, waged a war, managed domestic affairs, secured peace, and contracted alliances.

The records kept of the printing accounts were scanty,

and only a few of them have survived.[7] This is not surprising. Congress moved from city to city, Secretary
Thomson had trouble with his baggage, it is remarkable
that not more was lost. Frequently there was no money;
in the years after peace no printer could hope to make a
profit by contracting with the Confederation Congress.
Routines of payment, when there did happen to be
money, were awkward. The printer submitted his bill to
the President, who was likely this year to be a person
different from last year; the President signed an order to
the treasurers—the joint treasurers first, then the Treasury
office—and they paid over the sums due. Sometimes
Congress "directed" a document to be published in the
newspapers as the only way it could be published at
all. And at least once, newspaper publication *not* authorized by Congress preceded the official authorized
issue of a document in separate form. Dr. Julian Boyd
particularly describes this episode in Volume VII of his
Jefferson Papers. The report of the Grand Committee
concerning coinage, written by Jefferson, was published
in 100 copies by Dunlap on June 2, 1785. Previously,
it had appeared in a newspaper—*The Providence Gazette* of July 24, 1784—with this note from the anony-
mous contributor, who must have been either Congressman David Howell or Governor Jabez Bowen himself,
addressed to the publisher John Carter:

Mr. Carter,
    The following plan, for a MONEY-MINT, &c., was sent
among other communications to the State, by its late Delegates in Congress. —It was shewn to several members of
Congress, and met with their approbation; but the author
of it being sent abroad on public business, and an adjourn-

ment coming on, no measures were taken thereon. —By its being published in your Gazette the next Congress may avail itself of the sentiments of the *virtuosi* on this subject.

The most unsatisfactory precedent, certainly, was the way the Old Congress had kept its journal. From the beginning, in '74, Thomson had determined to record no debates, no discussion, only decisions taken and the yeas and nays on them. "What Congress adopted, I committed to writing," Thomson explained; "with what they rejected, I had nothing farther to do." The *Journal*, in consequence, was merely a skeleton. Its annual printing history is a very complicated bibliographical story, involving several printers—Dunlap, Claypoole, Aitken, Patterson—and when the monthly *Journals* begin, in that brief revival of Congressional vitality in 1779, and then the weekly *Journals* immediately afterwards, the bibliographical story becomes, we must admit, overloaded with "points," even for those of us who enjoy such intricacies. Because not enough copies were printed, few Americans knew precisely what the acts of Congress were. After a while, few really cared. Unhappily, the precedent of this kind of a journal was one which the houses of Congress of the new government adopted apparently without questioning its value. Senate and House journals remained, for years after 1789, the same sort of bare skeleton Charles Thomson had first articulated.

But I do not mean to ignore nor detract from the value of Old Congress documents. The collector could find some enchantment in them. There is Aitken's *Bible* of 1782, encouraged by an authorizing resolution of Congress which gave it an official status; it was the first

Bible published in the English language in the New World. Dearden and Watson in 1930 located thirty-two copies. There is Aitken's *Journal of Congress* from January to May, 1776, an octavo of 237 pages, very hard to come by today, because in April, just before Aitken bound up his monthly parts in a volume, Congress ordered him to use a different, smaller type, and to set the entire year's *Journal* over again. He had already marketed eighty copies of his stock on hand; The Historical Society of Pennsylvania has one of the few sold. All the rest Aitken was obliged to destroy, so they would not compete with the next printing. The canny Scot took the whole supply, fourteen reams of printed paper, and sold it to Benjamin Flower as wadding for cartridges for the army at thirty shillings a ream.[8]

Aitken was not the principal printer to Congress, and the only personal anecdote I know about him constrains me not to like him very much, but his manuscript account book and his "Waste Book" at The Library Company of Philadelphia are a real help in discovering exactly what he printed for the delegates, how many copies of each item he issued, and how he served them as stationer, bookseller, even as shipper of their libraries and papers. On September 18, 1776, we note, he billed the "Congress Navy board" for printing "a broad sheet Demy 500 Articles for Vessels of war, & paper," £3-15. This was one of those early exceptions I mentioned, an example of an adminstrative committee contracting printing on its own budget, not through Secretary Thomson of the whole Congress. Aitken also billed "Congress for War Office" for twelve copies of the *Journals* at 7/6 a copy; Congress itself for fifty copies at 7/6; he bound up two copies of the Bradfords' and his *Journals* together in one set in boards for Charles Thomson, at Congress' expense.

The principal printers to Congress were John Dunlap and David C. Claypoole, over a number of years. We have seen how Dunlap, with no press of his own in New York, contracted with John M'Lean for printing the new Constitution. On another occasion, also in New York in 1787, General Henry Knox of the War Office wanted one hundred fifty copies of the *Rules and Articles for the Government of the Troops.* He had John Swaine of New York print them. This would have been one of those independent administrative issues, except for the fact that Knox had no money to spend. And so Swaine billed, not Congress, but Congress' printer, Dunlap. And Dunlap in turn sent his account in to Congress, charging £2-4 for the hundred fifty *Rules* Swaine had printed.

The manuscript "Register of Accounts" includes also the protest, in that vigorous year 1779, by the Commissioners of Accounts, that the printer Claypoole is charging Congress far too much for his work, "in almost every article." The Commissioners urge Congress to take printing bids every three months, and choose the smallest bidder. Meanwhile, they say, go ahead and pay Claypoole twelve thousand dollars on account. Steiner and Cist, likewise, have been extravagant in their charges. You will find this protest printed in the notes to the *Journals of the Continental Congress,* Volume XV, pages 1462-63. Congress did appoint inspectors of the press, and awarded them on March 5, 1781 five thousand dollars for contingent expenses (*Journals,* XIX, p.

231). But little improvement resulted in the handling of printing contracts. Moving about from city to city as it did, Congress was at the mercy of the printers, or of their own Philadelphia procurer of printing. The "Register of Accounts" lists numerous items, printed by Dunlap, Dunlap and Claypoole, Francis Childs, or others, or bound up by the Philadelphia binder Robert Hodge, which are not known today. The *Journals* reproduce fragments of this tantalizing document for several years (XXIX, p. 931; XXX, p. 969, and the places previously cited).

For reasons not unconnected with loyalty and warguilt problems in the history of our own times, I should like to own for myself copies of the loyalty oaths Congress printed. And I should like a broadside of February 23, 1782, announcing that Congress refuses to exchange the prisoner Charles, Earl Cornwallis, "not from any apprehension of his influence or superior abilities, but because they look on him not in the light of a British General but a barbarian." Collectors should not consider it uninteresting to acquire the first printing of the North West Ordinance, or the Land Ordinance of 1785: these are among our definitive statements of what Americanism is, and what liberty. They are part of our heritage of freedom. Western collectors should prize also two broadsides of June 20, 1788, on George Morgan's memorial respecting "a tract of land in the Illinois country, on the Mississippi."

Cole describes the Church copy of the Articles of Confederation, the second draft, printed under that imposing rule of secrecy of July 12, 1776, which we noted in our first lecture. Church did not have, but a collector of American national Americana might well look for, that other document printed under the same strict impediment of secrecy at that same time, the first month of Independence, by Dunlap, in eighty copies. It is the five-page folio *Plan of Treaties*, the very first statement by the architects of our Independence on the means and manners by which we should conduct ourselves as a nation in a world of nations. One of the wonders of '76 was the way a Boston lawyer, Adams, a Virginia planter, Harrison, a Philadelphia merchant, Robert Morris, the printer Benjamin Franklin, a Pennsylvania advocate, John Dickinson, with no previous experience of diplomacy, could chart a practical course for embassies, consulates, and ministries out of the books of Sully, Pufendorf, Grotius, Castiglioni, Machiavelli, and Vattel.[9] Adams wrote the *Plan of Treaties*. It was a work of creative imagination, by a man who, you will remember, said of politics that he found no romance more exciting. It is the basis and the first formulation of the foreign relations of the United States. But I have never known a collector to seek it, a librarian to prize it, or rarely a historian to think it much worth his time.

Names associated with Old Congress documents read like a roll call of the patriots: Hancock, Washington, Jefferson, Adams, Hamilton, Dickinson, many others. The report on the health of soldiers is by Dr. Benjamin Rush; Thomas Hutchins comes honestly by his title, "geographer to the United States." There is appeal in these names.

But if I should be asked to pick, among all the things Congress published between the *Plan of Treaties* of 1776 and that little broadside of 1788 announcing the time for the new government to assemble, one item alone, which I might keep, in mint condition, as my favorite, I know what I should choose without an instant's hesitation. You will recall what I said about the *Rules for the Government of the Troops,* first published on June 30, 1775, and issued in frequent reprints and revisions for twenty years and more thereafter— that it was the beginning of our constitutional structure, the earliest description of national powers, the basis of our law of war. Well, to go along with it, for actual training and drilling of men, all the army at first had were the innumerable American reprints of British military instructors, particularly Harvey's *The Manual Exercise as Ordered by His Majesty in 1764,* or amateurish copies of that famous handbook made for colonial units, such as the *Easy Plan of Discipline for a Militia,* a manual composed by Lieutenant Timothy Pickering of the Essex County (Massachusetts) Volunteers, in 1775. Designed to replace these insufficient guides and provide a standardized national training came in 1779 another book, a strange one, perhaps, to pick as a favorite, but a book with a rich association around it, and perhaps—I am not sure, but perhaps— the most often reprinted book that Congress issued. Someone could have a grand time and make a real contribution to our knowledge by assembling in one collection all the many editions it has gone through. It was called *Regulations for the Order and Discipline of the Troops of the United States. Part I,* published by Styner and Cist in Second street, Philadelphia, in 1779, a duodecimo of 154 numbered pages plus nine unfoliated, with eight plates. If collectors ever turn to the field of

American government documents, this first *Regulations* will be regarded as one of the most engaging and valuable pieces of Americana.

In the awesome ordeal of Valley Forge there was one Falstaffian figure of comic relief, the hearty, courageous, hard-living, profane, energetic German, something faintly spurious about him, perhaps, something ridiculous about his inability to learn English, a wonderful hilarity about his braying and ranting obscenely at the troops, faithfully attended all the while by his huge greyhound Azor; yet nothing but skill and craftsmanship in the way he converted American militiamen into the model of an Army. Washington had a rough farmer's relish of this rough, vigorous man. He secured the appointment of Major General the Baron Friedrich Wilhelm August Heinrich Ferdinand von Steuben as Inspector General of the troops. And von Steuben worked with amazing effect.

To help him drill Americans, he had four aides. Two he brought with him from abroad: Chevalier the Viscomte Louis de Fleury was one; [10] another was a tiny little man, who peered myopically through the thickest lenses anyone had ever seen, Captain Pierre Etienne DuPonceau. Little Captain DuPonceau had the English; he first met von Steuben in Paris, crossed the Atlantic with him to be his translator. They made an odd appearance together, drilling the troops at Valley Forge, the enormous bawdy Prussian and the scholarly little mite of a French *literateur*. It is told how, much later, Captain DuPonceau lost his glasses on the field of Monmouth, became confused, but being a genuinely spirited military character galloped nonetheless into battle—

alas! at the head not of his own American but of a
British company of hussars. The story is only a legend,
as were many other tales of his nearsightedness and
absent-mindedness,[11] but it is certainly truth that Peter
Stephen DuPonceau, as he came to call himself, emerged
after the war as one of the most original and successful
of American lawyers, founder of the Law Academy of
Philadelphia, brilliant pleader before the Supreme
Court, statesman and philosopher, lifelong opponent of
the Common Law, advocate, instead, of the democratic
processes of a legislatively enacted code, leader and bene-
factor of the public institutions of Philadelphia.[12]

Von Steuben's third aide was for American liaison,
Captain Benjamin Walker, French-speaking, English-
born, now a resident of New York. Von Steuben got
him from Washington's "family." To Walker, incidentally, General Washington spoke one of the few
jokes he is ever known to have made. And when von
Steuben began to prepare his drill manual, he needed
a fourth—someone to draw pictures, that everyone might
understand what his directions meant. Around the Valley Forge encampment was a destitute young French-
man who occupied his time making crayon portraits of
officers and their wives. The Prussian Inspector seized
upon him. He was a real artist: his father was Painter
in Ordinary to King Louis at his Manufactory of the
Gobelin Tapestries on the Rue St. Hippolyte in Paris;
he himself had studied military art under his father at
the Royal Academy, drawing imaginary battle scenes
from the Old Testament books of Chronicles and Kings.
He was Pierre Charles L'Enfant, and von Steuben's assignment was the first real work he did as an American

officer. One day he would design forts and emplacements; later would be New York City's principal Federal architect; finally he would create, as his permanent monument, his city in the wilderness, Washington, D.C.

As soon as Howe evacuated Philadelphia and the American army moved into the city from Valley Forge, von Steuben called his staff together and commenced work on his "system of discipline and military exercises." He himself wrote, Colonel Fleury assisted, DuPonceau "translated and copied," Walker edited, L'Enfant drew the eight plates for, General Washington read over and approved, the drill manual of 1779. Colonel Timothy Pickering corrected the proof sheets. America's first Army handbook was thus made by a Prussian tactician, three Frenchmen, and an American liaison. Congress, in this year of its revived energy, made an entry on its journal: [13]

A letter of the 25th from baron Steuben was read, accompanied with a system of regulation for the infantry of the United States; also a letter from the board of war, representing that baron Steuben, inspector general, has formed a system of exercise and discipline for the infantry of the United States: that the same has been submitted to the inspection of the commander in chief, and his remarks thereon and amendments incorporated in the work; that it has been examined with attention by the board, and is highly approved, as being calculated to produce important advantages to the states; and therefore praying "that it may receive the sanction of Congress and be committed to the press;" whereupon . . .

Ordered, That the board of war cause as many copies thereof to be printed as they shall deem requisite for the use of the troops.

STEUBEN'S MANUAL OF MILITARY DISCIPLINE

(Copy in The Library Company of Philadelphia)

One of Major L'Enfant's eight plates illustrating von Steuben's *Regulations for the Order and Discipline of the Troops,* from the first Philadelphia issue of 1779. In addition to all the others who had a hand in preparing the manual, John Laurens and Alexander Hamilton both did some polishing of the final version. Steuben wrote, not in his own language which was German, but in French. When shown the English translation he could understand not a word of it, but had to memorize the English commands and rehearse them before his staff. Soldiers at Valley Forge frequently failed to understand his peculiar pronunciation or his shoutings in French and German, but militia captains everywhere understood his book, and by its precepts the American army was formed, trained, and administered.

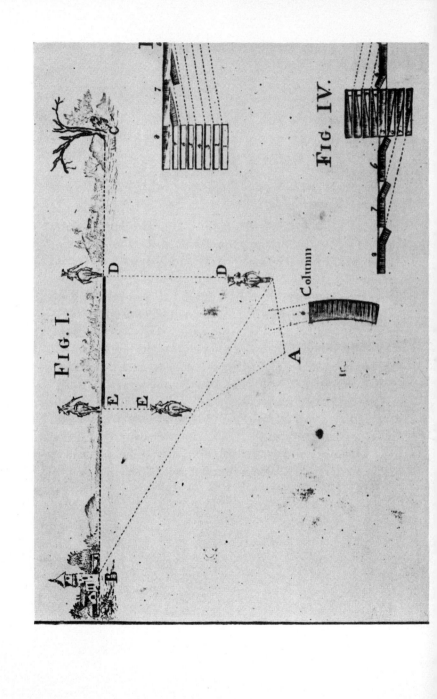

Now we take especial notice of that last part of the order, for here is Congress in 1779 specifically delegating to a board the responsibility of dealing with the printer, and publishing as many copies as it wishes. This is another of those early exceptions I spoke of, another of the examples of publication by an administrative unit instead of by Congress itself.

Actually, Congress need not have feared the manual would be neglected. Folks at home wanted to know what army life was like, and just as the earlier *Rules for the Government of the Troops* had been, so this drill manual was reprinted at once in many places. States, too, adopted it: before 1779 was over, Pennsylvania had issued *An Abstract of a System of Military Discipline: Framed by the Hon. the Baron Steuben* for the use of its own battalions of state militia.

Finally, the statesmen in New York in 1789 could trace in the issues of the Old Congress the development of the bones and sinews of government. Fail the Confederation did, but still we must acknowledge that if one government rose where formerly there had been thirteen, it was in large part because of the strengths, not the weaknesses of the Confederation Congress. Steadily, the delegates had shown the duties and services a single central government could perform. Not for very long after the summer of '75 did the Old Congress have to rely on the Pennsylvania delegates to execute their actions, or request state conventions and Philadelphia city committees to do their chores for them. In November, 1775, a foreign service was set up of agents and correspondents, and a Congressional Committee established to keep in touch with them. Soon Congress itself was fractionated in a congeries of committees.[14] Throughout the fifteen years of war and Confederacy these committees were reformed, reshaped, and described. In '77, printed resolutions re-established the Commissary Department, the Quartermaster Department, the Treasury Committee; a Board of War emerged, and a Naval Committee; in '80 the Inspector's Department and the Hospital Department were set up; throughout the period the Post Office Department was revised and expanded, and the Land Office, and the Treasury; the Secretary's office was remodeled, the "five great departments" as they came to be called were restudied, the "Grand Committee" was erected to act when a quorum failed to attend. Each of the executive departments was described in official publications. Court martial trials were published (in surprisingly few copies each, incidentally—100 of Charles Lee's, 100 of St. Clair's, 50 only of Benedict Arnold's); and in 1778 Congress even published the first work in historical investigation to be issued by the American government: *Observations on the American Revolution. Published according to a resolution of Congress, by their Committee. For the Consideration of those who are desirous of comparing the Conduct of the opposed Parties, and The several Consequences* which have flowed from it, 8vo, 122 plus (4) p., Styner & Cist, a publication which, since historians are never free of people to tell them how to do the thing they have done better, was immediately attacked by the irresponsible Thomas Paine, in *Common Sense.*

It could not have escaped the attention of the statesmen of 1789 that David C. Claypoole, even before he combined with Dunlap, had called himself repeatedly on his title page, "Printer to the Honourable the Congress of the United States." It was a title that brought Claypoole little honor and less profit; but it, too, was a precedent which would be followed under the New Roof of the Federal Edifice.

No testimony more humble but more convincing could be advanced of the renewed vitality of the national government after Washington took his presidential oath on the balcony of New York's Federal Hall in April, '89, than the increase in the printing activities of the government. That year of public debate, 1788, the year of the Ratification Controversy, had been a year of public education. Now, the people wanted to know what their government did. They demanded to know. As Madison left home for his seat in the House of Representatives, he received a letter from his neighbor, Elder John Leland: [15]

I expect that Congress will be very busy for some Years, in filling a continental Blank with a Code of General Laws; and I think it will be very Judicious to send those Laws very liberally into the States, that Eyes may always be open. No Danger of the Destruction of Liberty when the community is well informed. Ignorance always brings on, either Mutiny or Lethargy, which equally pave the way for Tyranny. . . . One Thing I shall expect; that if religious Liberty is anywise threatened, that I shall receive the earliest Intelligence.

All Madison's colleagues agreed with him and with Elder Leland about publication. The details of how Congress published and recorded for the people take us into the organization of the two houses of the new legislative body.

Now the Papers of the House of Representatives, which have recently come into the National Archives, do not, unfortunately, for the first fourteen Congresses, contain very much of the Clerk's dealings with the printers. Noncurrent or noncontinuing records seem to have been destroyed, Clerks changed three times in this period, and the whole staff of the Clerk's office seems to have been eternally busy copying every kind of document into large folio books. Incredibly enough, scribes of the House even copied *printed* journals and papers in their fair clerkly hands into big ledgers. About the only useful things the bibliographer will find in the House of Representatives papers for 1789–1817 are the accounts of moneys paid out, including sums paid for printing, stationery, and supplies. They will help when occasionally they indicate the item printed; usually they merely settle the quarterly accounts rendered by the printers to the House Clerk. These quarterly accounts, when they turn up, sometimes prove to itemize the printing done by title and pages, and are of specific value. They should be made available to the scholar by reproduction in some form, somewhere.[16]

The Senate Papers, however, are a far different kind of record.[17] Though the National Archives staff has done its usual superb job of classifying, arranging, and preserving the Senate papers, historians have not yet discovered the riches contained in them. They will. For our purposes, the surviving corpus of housekeeping records of the Senate during the first fourteen Congresses, 1789–1817, is a cask of buried treasure. Till very near the end of this period of years, the Senate had the same Secretary, Mr. Samuel Allyne Otis, a man of mature years and precise habits, one of those Boston Federalist Otises, father of Harrison Gray Otis, proud of his job and his Senate, above all an excellent housekeeper, with that passion for detail which belongs to the clerkly mind. Clerks and bibliographers, be it noted, have much in common.

The office of the Secretary of the Senate was set up as an administrative unit separate from all else in the government. Otis was answerable only to his members, the Senators. Congress each year told the Treasury how much to pay him and his clerks on the Civil List, and how much of a contingent fund to give him. This contingent fund was $250 in October, 1789; it leapt to $2,300 the next March, 1790; it would steadily grow every year.[18] And on the Secretary, as on the Clerk of the House, devolved immediately the administration of legislative business.

The first month of our government, May 28, 1789, Congress passed a resolution leaving to the Secretary of the Senate and the Clerk of the House the responsibility of making printing contracts. They were directed to secure 600 copies of the *Acts* of each session, 700 copies of the *Journals* of each house, to be distributed to the members and to the executive, judiciary, and heads of the departments of the United States government, as well as the executive, legislative and judicial branches of every state.[19] This would practically exhaust the 600 and 700 copies, you will note, in official distribution, and leave none for public purchase. Printers in New York City were anxious for these govern-

ment printing contracts, not because they were particularly lucrative; they weren't. Rather, they were appeal-
ing for the inside track they would give to the printers
chosen for filling the columns of the newspapers most
of them published as their principal business, and for
serving the government in more profitable respects.

Francis Childs and John Swaine talked with Secretary Otis and John Beckley, Clerk of the House, as the
new government assembled. After negotiation, they engaged (June 9) to print the Laws of Congress (the *Acts*)
in 600 copies for a price of two and a half dollars for
every sheet of letter press, if the United States government would furnish the paper.[20] The retained copy of
their original contract has survived in the Senate papers.
Childs & Swaine were to be paid quarterly on rendering
accounts, at the rate of 20 shillings current money of
New York for each sheet of 600 copies of the *Acts*. They
were to execute the printing in a faithful and workmanlike manner, and if required were to put together
the 600 copies half-stitched.[21] A memorandum initialed
July 2 hired Childs & Swaine for the printing of the
Laws, "until further order." [22] For a long time, incidentally, the Secretary of the Senate and the Clerk of
the House from these contracts were in the business of
purchasing paper stocks. Secretary Otis bought his, while
the Congress sat in New York, from Henry Kammerer
of Philadelphia, with whom he exchanged some letters
that some day a happy historian of printing will delight
to publish.[23]

Having secured the printer for the *Acts,* Clerk Beckley and Secretary Otis drew up an agreement with each
other, on June 29, arranging that "for the greater con-

venience to themselves and Utility to the Public," Otis
should employ a printer for the *Journal* of the Senate,
Beckley a different printer for the *Journal* of the House;
they would consider Childs & Swaine joint employees
of both houses for the *Acts,* and jointly they would en-
gage Thomas Greenleaf for "other printing of Bills as
may be necessary from time to time for the use of the
Senate and House of Representatives of the United
States." [24]

Now employing Greenleaf for "other printing of
Bills as may be necessary" was the beginning of the so-
called "slip laws." The resolution of May 28 calling for
printed *Acts* of each session in 600 copies envisioned a
bound volume after Congress had adjourned. We call
these volumes "Session Laws" or "Pamphlet Laws" or,
as I am in the habit of saying for my period, from the
first word in the titles of all the volumes, simply the
"Acts." But Congress decided on two other courses of
action that determined how a law should be made by
this new government, how published abroad, how kept
in the records. The first was another joint resolution,
June 4-5, 1789, providing that within ten days of pas-
sage of any law, twenty-two copies of it should be lodged
with the President, who would send two copies to the
governor of each state. There were at that moment
eleven states, Rhode Island and North Carolina not yet
having ratified; hence the twenty-two copies. These
were the slip laws, the individual printings with no
title pages, index numbers, usually no session number
or even a Congress number to identify them. Slip laws
are still being published, and though in a huge edition,
they still do not bear numbers corresponding to the

chapter numbers they eventually assume in the Statutes at Large.

The second decision was a statute of September 15, 1789—the first American law about laws—which gave the Secretary of State custody of the original copy of each law passed, directed him to supply one printed copy of each to each Senator and Representative, and to secure the printing of each in three newspapers of general circulation. Keeping the original laws was the beginning of the Office of the Rolls in the State Department. Here the authentic, original law, signed by the President, reposed, and still reposes.

These two decisions called, you will observe, for slip-law printings in two quantities—the twenty-two copies for the President, the additional larger number of copies for the Secretary of State. The printers usually printed the smaller number on very fine paper, the larger on ordinary paper. And you will see from these provisions that the "other printing of Bills as may be necessary" was not a small part of the printing account.

Thomas Greenleaf was the obvious man for the "other printing" business, for he was the printer Otis had chosen for the Senate *Journals*. In this contract, Otis engaged Greenleaf in the business of printing the *Journal* "until further order, upon condition that he performs it, in a Workmanlike manner, and deliver the same, pressed, folded and half stitched to my order, and for which he is to be allowed and paid by the United States, two Dollars and an half for every Sheet of the Journals of four pages and in that proportion for other printing." [25]

Greenleaf took the job. His account for the first session lists how many sheets of paper he has used for each imprint: from 25 sheets each for such items as the Ohio Act, the Light House Bill, or the Act for Keeping the Seal, to 360 sheets for the Act to Punish Crimes, or 1,480 sheets for the Judiciary Bill, of which he printed 370 copies on four and a half sheets each.[26] These slip laws were "other printing"; though he was setting the *Journals* of the Senate and delivering them each week,[27] as he had contracted, the separate acts of the Senate became even in this first session a bigger part of his official service.

He even did some "other printing" for the House, too, whose *Journal* along with the *Acts* belonged by Beckley's contract to Childs & Swaine. Greenleaf printed the budget estimate in July, and the proposal of the first ten amendments (the Bill of Rights) for the House separately from the Senate.[28] These first ten amendments, since they were Congress acts, were printed for the two houses independently of each other, and President Washington, accustomed to sending the slip laws in two copies to each governor, apparently submitted the action of both houses on the amendments separately to each state in the same fashion. Nothing in Article V prescribed exactly how it should be done.

Childs & Swaine meanwhile had separately printed the first Copyright Bill, which Noah Webster had written, the first Tariff Bill, the Act establishing the War Department, the Ohio Act (which Greenleaf separately issued, though Evans does not list his printing), an Indian Treaty Act, a Pension Act, and a Tonnage Act. Both printers, as their bills prove, published items nowhere listed in bibliographies.[29]

Evans notes, with a somewhat puzzled tone, that all the separate broadside acts of 1789–91 in the New York Public Library are printed on writing paper and have the words "[True Copy]" or "Deposited among the Rolls in the Office of the Secretary of State," and a space where Secretary Jefferson has signed each. Copies on ordinary paper do not have this legend.[30] Evans need not have worried. This was just the result of that second resolution calling for two slip laws to go to each governor, and that first law about laws directing the Secretary of State to send a printed (not necessarily a signed) copy to each Senator and Representative. The *Checklist* would have explained it all to Evans, had he bothered to consult it. But bibliographers never seem to consult it.

As a matter of practice, Otis or Beckley frequently sent the slip laws to states, just as they did the final *Acts* of each session. At first, governors, speakers of assemblies, presidents of state senates would write proper thank-you letters to Otis for the receipt of the slip laws, or the final bound volume of *Acts*. They did so during the first three Congresses,[31] but by and by they stopped bothering, and after a few years no more such polite acknowledgments from the states were received. On the whole, states saved scarcely any of these official copies. I have seen some slip laws in the Archives at Concord, New Hampshire, but have sometimes enquired elsewhere in vain.

As the First Congress' second session began in December, 1789, Secretary Otis received the first of the many letters of application that would come to him over the years. This one was from Samuel Loudon, printer, of No. 5 Water St., New York, "near the Old Slip," who had heard the Secretary had been given the choice of a printer, and promised that if chosen he would do the work with accuracy and dispatch. "I could offer some reasons for my participating in a share of the public printing," Loudon wrote, ". . . but I forbear, lest they might be misconstrued as proceeding from an invidious mind." [32] Otis did dismiss Greenleaf, but not for Loudon. He used John Fenno for the weekly Senate *Journal* in 1790, and before the government moved to Philadelphia in the autumn had paid Fenno $450.50 for binding as well. Benjamin Larkin shared the binding contracts. Fenno's itemized bill for the second session, including his binding, shows 700 copies of the *Journals* at 80 cents per sheet, 26 separate acts and reports amounting to seven sheets and 19 half sheets, stitching 373 sets of the *Journals* in blue paper covers. The total was $862.82.[33] Evans lists none of the twenty-six bills and reports Fenno emitted; only some of them are catalogued in Greely. Many of them doubtless exist.

Childs & Swaine continued to print for the House during 1790. One of their imprints was Secretary of War Knox's brilliant first report, *A Plan for the General Arrangement of the Militia of the United States,* three hundred copies of which were ordered, not by Knox, but by the House of Representatives.[34] Reports of State, Treasury, Postmaster General, Attorney General, even presidential proclamations were on Clerk Beckley's or Secretary Samuel Allyne Otis' printing bills, as were at least four different editions of Jefferson's report on Weights, Measures, and Coinage. These were executive documents being printed by Congress. Departments independently for a long time printed nothing but forms and circulars, and even these they frequently issued through the Congress, to be paid for on Otis' or Beckley's accounts.

The bound volumes of the *Acts* of Congress, issued at the end of each session by Childs & Swaine, were sometimes reprinted by other presses in the first few years of the new government. But soon the appeal of them to commercial printers ceased, as Congressional legislation became more familiar, less exciting news, and reprints stopped. Bound *Acts* came to be very hard to get. They were always in short supply. Six hundred copies barely covered the official distribution, left few for the general public, few for the Congressmen themselves. That is probably one reason why Clerk Beckley's assistants were set to copying printed laws into the manuscript ledger books by hand. Senators could never find copies of the printings for their own use, neither could cabinet officers nor lesser departmental officials. When he set up office in Philadelphia the clerk of the State Department had only one single copy of the *Acts* for 1790.[35]

Soon, the Secretary of State was given general direction of the republication of the laws in not three, but five "newspapers of general circulation." Secretary Jefferson thought this arrangement "altogether too partial and too perishable," and of course the selection of the newspaper printers quickly became a partisan political issue. Secretary Timothy Pickering, redoubtable Federalist though he was, did select the Republican Freneau (Philip Freneau's brother) to publish the laws in South Carolina, but later when he needed a Kentucky contractor, General Pickering wrote to a western Federalist to find him in Kentucky a printer, known "for correctness in typography, intelligence, and *real,* not boasting & *professing,* patriotism"—which was about as close as Tim Pick could come to a definition of the True Faith.[36]

When the government moved to Philadelphia, Mr. Secretary Otis of the Senate had to adjust to new printers. They gave him some trouble, particularly since by the third year of the new government the process of legislation had advanced to that state of complexity in which Senate and House both had to have the successive stages of a bill printed for the members during the debates concerning it. Pressures of time, reminiscent of the Bradfords' achievements back in '74, or Dunlap's printing of the July 5, 1776 broadside Declaration, or Dunlap and Claypoole's printing of the September 17th Constitution, became regular problems of the government contractors. At the Clements Library I was shown a set, beautifully preserved in fresh, original condition, of the stages of a bill relating to the Michigan area, in one of the 1790 Congresses. The set included the committee report, printed, with lines numbered in the margin; the bill as reported after debate from the committee of the whole, printed; and the bill as adopted, printed. This last was not yet the slip law; it was still in one house only. They made three separate publication items. Librarians do not always know what to do with these surviving curiosities. A genuine interest in the printing history of the government and in the legislative processes of democracy would dictate the terms of their preservation and cataloguing. Sometimes successive stages of a bill turn up in personal papers of members.

They are part of the essential history of legislation, they are often unlisted government imprints, they frequently can be dated even to the day on which they were set up and impressed, they are important revelations of the printing practices of the period.

Some of these reports and second readings had to be composed and impressed overnight. Haste of this sort began to be routine during the first session held in Philadelphia. In February, 1791, Secretary Otis received a letter from Tobias Lear, who signed even this hurried communication in his proud style, "Secretary to the President of the United States": [37]

Sir [wrote Tobias Lear], I will thank you to send me, from time to time, two Copies of such bills as may be printed by order of the Senate, previous to their passing into laws; and likewise two copies of your Journals as they are printed.

I am induced to make this request from a wish which the President of the United States often expresses to see bills in this Stage.

Otis had such trouble getting the preliminary printings furnished for his own Senators that it is doubtful if he could very often oblige the President. The President, for his part, declined to oblige the Senate Secretary in this same hard problem of printing time. Just before the 1792 session of the Second Congress opened, Mr. Otis sent an earnest request to Washington, which Lear answered politely on November 5: [38]

I mentioned to the President your desire to have a copy of his Speech the day before he should meet Congress, in order to enable you to furnish the printers (who are pressing on such occasions) and to facilitate your official arrangements

in the commencements of the session. The President upon
considering the matter thought it might not be proper to
let a copy go out before he delivered it, lest he should see
occasion to make some alterations before he delivered it.

The printers had other matters to complain of besides
the pressure of time. Pay was slow. In March, 1794, Otis
was still trying to get the Treasury to pay John Dunlap's
account of $237 for his work in 1792 and '93.[39] In the
spring of 1795, John Fenno was late with the *Journal*.
"The work spins out beyond expectation," he wrote
Otis. "I have upwards of 100 pages finished—expect the
whole will be about 150. Had ten hands on it last Sunday
& have ten today. My son thinks we can get a number
finished on Tuesday—Have done no other work since it
came into the office—& hope you will not be disap-
pointed." [40]

Under pressures of time, Fenno sometimes found his
"ten hands" insufficient, and occasionally he would farm
out work to other printers. When yellow fever emptied
Philadelphia in the fall and winter of 1793 he had to
turn to others, had to turn wherever he could find workmen. Robert Aitken's *Waste Book* in The Library Company tells this story in laconic entries: Aitken bills
Fenno during November and December for printing
the President's speech, "broadside Demy 60 Copies";
and for printing seventy-five copies of a circular letter,
two hundred copies of the "State of the Ballances in
hands of Supervisors," and five hundred sets of bills of
exchange for the bank. Aitken, and Andrew Brown of
the *Federal Gazette,* were the only printers who stayed
at work during the plague. One of the few civil servants
who stayed at work was Joshua Dawson, treasury clerk

in the Register's Office, and during the plague Aitken prints for the Register's office directly, not through Fenno nor through Secretary Otis or Clerk Beckley, forms and certificates, thus:

Nov. 9. Reg.ʳ Office D.ʳ

To printˢ	960	Emrollmᵗˢ @ 6/	2	.. 17	.. 6
To d.ᵒ	960	Recordˢ Vessels	2	.. 17	.. 6
To d.ᵒ	960	License und.ʳ 20 Tons	2	.. 17	.. 6
To d.ᵒ	960	d.ᵒ above d.ᵒ	2	.. 17	.. 6

                                         11 .. 8

It is a significant indication how bad the plague was that Scottish Mr. Aitken added up his figures in that account incorrectly, and cheated himself of two shillings.

Careless workmen or boys could lose time and even lose copy or proof in delivery.[41] Fenno complained of that; and Otis always wanted the *Journal* delivered daily, whether it made a whole sheet or not. His sharp criticisms sometimes stung Fenno. "I sent the Sheets uncorrected because you gave orders by Maxwell [Otis' clerk] to Hyde [the binder], that they should only be folded," Fenno wrote the Secretary at the end of 1797. "All the Copy we now have in Hand is composed, except the single sheet rec.ᵈ this day. It will often happen that the Copy we have will not fill a half sheet in 8vo form—this will render it impossible to furnish one daily, unless it is sent in partly blank. I am not indifferent about doing the work—and believe I feel as anxious as anyone you could employ to give satisfaction."[42] The harassed printer knew too well that the Bostonian Federalist Secretary was being courted by his Philadelphia

DOCUMENTS ON THE WAR
WITH FRANCE

(Elkins Copy, Free Library of Philadelphia)

The House of Representatives had William Ross print a thick quarto volume containing all the documents relating to the Naval War with France, which was just beginning in 1797. This is the title page of the Elkins Copy, an uncut example in contemporary binding. It was the work of which Secretary of State Pickering complained, as inconvenient and hasty, and improperly paged because Ross had farmed out the printing among half a dozen shops. In his own haste, Secretary Pickering failed to notice the printer's error on the title page ("witih" for "With") which was never corrected.

A

MESSAGE

FROM THE

PRESIDENT

OF THE

UNITED STATES OF AMERICA,

TO

Congress;

RELATIVE TO THE

FRENCH REPUBLIC;

DELIVERED JANUARY 19, 1797,

WITH

THE PAPERS THEREIN REFERRED TO.

Published by Order of the House of Representatives.

PHILADELPHIA:

PRINTED BY W. ROSS, NEAR CONGRESS-HALL.

competition: by Poulson, and Oswald, and John Bring-
hurst with his new press; by Way & Groff who were
moving to better quarters, and who had already received
some business from the Secretary.[43]

Even after the *Journals* were delivered to the printer
each year and Congress had finished its session and
recessed, there was editing to do, an index to make,
errata to note, and addenda, and always an Indian treaty
or two to include before the *Acts* could be bound up.[44]
This Otis invariably wanted done before he went home
to Boston for the summer. Sometimes Mr. Secretary had
complaints of printing standards. To John Ward Fenno
he wrote brusquely in January, 1800,[45]

Sir,
    Sheet G of the Journals of S appears to have been done
with an old type & inferior paper.
    The unequal distances of words also gives the work a less
pleasing appearance.
    I send you a sheet of the journals of S & of the H of R
that you may see the difference in printing & paper.

And sometimes, since this was government printing,
the inevitable political issues appeared. Secretary of
State Timothy Pickering scolded the House for its way
of publishing critical documents on the tense wartime
relations with France, and he turned to the Senate. He
demanded to see proof sheets of the Senate's imprint of
his letter to Pinckney, requested Otis to have Fenno
bring the sheets to his office. When he saw them, he
wrote Otis,[46]

The measures for printing the documents relative to
French Affairs have been taken with so much precipitation,

the publication will appear in a very inconvenient form. The documents were distributed by the printer for the House, among half a dozen printers, and each began marking their own pages without any relation to the others. To remedy in some measure this confusion, I have numbered all the documents handed to the Senate, in a regular series, and without these, we cannot number those sent to the House which are now so dispersed, and which have no numbers. I wish therefore to be indulged with the use of those belonging to the Senate. The whole will in a short time be printed. Perhaps when seen the Senate may direct a more convenient edition for themselves, in the manner in which M<u>r</u> Fenno is printing the letter to Mr. Pinckney.

And once—only once—a government printer embarrassed the Senate by an inaccurate announcement. It happened by accident, as Fenno explained: [47] he was sorry he printed in his newspaper that William Vans Murray had been appointed minister to "the Republic of Batavia." He copied it from a competing newspaper, the *New World,* which had been published about an hour before he went to press; he had not received the information from any senator.

Politics were tense in this time of the French War and the Alien and Sedition Acts. The Philadelphia printers were in the midst of the partisan struggle. Against one of them, Republican William Duane, Federalist Mr. Otis' Federalist Senate brought contempt proceedings, commanded him to the bar of the house, charged him with a "high breach of the privileges of the Senate." [48] One might have thought Duane's chances of Senate printing contracts were over forever, one may imagine Mr. Otis wished they were. But he was to have quite a lot to do with William Duane before many years had passed.

In the Philadelphia period, Senate binding was done by George Hyde. I cannot find any other bills than his; there may have been some which are lost. His bills were for binding, stitching, and delivery; to handle his accounts rendered is almost to be there with him in his shop: [49]

1796. June 1th. 130 Copies to Sig X stitched in blue.
1796. July 6. 60 Copies stitch.d in blue N.B. 30 of them to Mr Fenno, & 30 to Office.
1796. Nov. 23. 160 Do, 1/2 Bound.

And so on, and a note such as this appended:

There is wanting to Complete 49 Books now on hand, 1 sheet of B, 3 sheets of D, 1 of H, 5 of N, 24½ of O, 3 of P, & 8½ of S. (There is a Number of Sheets of the last part over).

Of all the government printed during its ten years in Philadelphia, we may well believe much is still to be listed. Childs & Swaine had moved to the city and were printing the folio slip laws for the Congress as they had in New York. They brought out Hamilton's famous financial reports, all the other executive communications including the one item which seems to have attracted collectors, the 1790 census; they bound up the *Acts* and *Journal of the House* at the end of each session; grimly they printed the annual accounts of receipts and expenditures on fine handmade paper. In 1794, a printed list they published gives sixty-five acts passed in the first session of the Third Congress, and seven resolutions.[50] It was only part of their work.

By 1792 a few more documents seem to be going to the printers directly from executive departments—such as Knox's directions for invalid pensioners [51]—but the printers they go to are still the Congressional printers, and many of them are charged on the quarterly bills rendered by the official contractors. In 1793, Secretary of the Treasury Hamilton publicly and bitterly complained that his communications had been inaccurately printed by the House; the Representatives cheerfully passed a resolution recommending that Secretary Hamilton order three hundred copies of his Report to be printed under his own direction. Hamilton did so; he had it done by the Senate printer Fenno. [52]

John Swaine died in November, 1794, a young man of thirty-two. Francis Childs continued alone with his *Daily Advertiser* in New York and the print shop in Philadelphia where his government contracts were. But Fenno, the Senate printer, was doing more House work under the "other printing" arrangement each year: in 1794 the accounts of receipts and expenditures, a House document, came from his press instead of Childs'; [53] he usually did the reports of the commissioners of the sinking fund, and usually presidential messages and proclamations. Childs, when Swaine's name dropped from his imprint, began to put on his title pages the legend, "Printed by Francis Childs, Printer of the Laws of the United States," an epithet he certainly was entitled to under the contracts of 1789, but which he used only this near the end of his governmental career.

The unauthorized printing of the Jay treaty, by Bache in Philadelphia in July, 1795, and by many printers immediately after, is a strange circumstance, [54] but equally strange is the fact no one has noticed that apparently neither official printer, Fenno nor Childs, published the treaty at all in an authorized issue until 1796, and then it was the House printer Childs instead of the Senate's Fenno.[55] At least, Childs's is the copy that is known. Probably Fenno printed it too, as well as all other foreign affairs and treaty messages which are now known only from Childs's imprints. In this and in other matters, Evans lists indiscriminately so many reprints of all sorts, the most frequent being schedules of import rates and drawbacks issued by printers everywhere, along with his correctly listed but thinly representative official documents by the authorized printers, that an unfortunate confusion emerges from his pages. Buried away in his items, however, are certain official documents not from Childs or Fenno, not even from Philadelphia presses, which *were* official government documents. One such was the address of the militia commander to the inhabitants of Pennsylvania, during the Whiskey Rebellion, a broadside printed by Scull at Pittsburgh in 1794.[56]

And certain other items went outside the official contracts, too. The first Folwell edition of the *Laws of the United States,* in two volumes, 1796, was actually ordered by Congress;[57] the Solomon Cotton *Collection of the Speeches of the President,* Boston, 1796, was not.[58] But in 1796 a third official printer appeared, to take some of Childs's and some of Fenno's work. William Ross of Philadelphia, "near Congress Hall," printed eight separate circulars that year relating to commerce on the seas, privateers, impressment, and duties. They were government documents, but which House ordered them, if either did, I do not know.[59] The Naval War with France was making everything move faster, and Ross was edging into the "other printing" area, where Greenleaf once had been. In addition to his circulars, he printed instructions on land warrant surveys that grew out of the Land Ordinance of 1785; [60] a House document on appropriations that ordinarily would have gone to Childs's shop,[61] a circular to United States marshals on how to keep their accounts that plainly was ordered printed by the Treasury department directly.[62]

By the next year, 1797, Ross was a steady part of the printing picture. He replaced Childs as printer of the *Acts,* with the beginning of the Fifth Congress (the Folwell edition of *these* session laws seems to have been a separate order of the House),[63] and that year also he issued the slip laws. Fenno continued to publish occasional House documents as well as his Senate work, but Ross took over all of Childs's work on the *Journal* of the House. This year, '97, too, saw the first official documents published by Joseph Gales, who would one day be a famous government printer in Washington. His maiden efforts were a committee report for the House on a pension for the daughters of the Compte de Grasse,[64] the report of the Mint, and the *Rules* of the House of Representatives.[65] To Fenno, however, went the honor of publishing the seven-page *Rules* for the Senate, written by the Vice President: this is the modest first edition of a great and important work, Jefferson's *Manual of Parliamentary Practice.*[66]

Ross was as busy as Childs had ever been. It was he whom Pickering described as farming out the work of the French relations to six different shops. One of these

shops may have been Gales's; another was probably
Zachariah Poulson's, for Poulson printed for the House
in 1797 the annual Treasury estimates for the fiscal
year,[67] the report of the commissioners of the sinking
fund,[68] and a War Department document.[69]

Folwell, Poulson, Gales—the old contracts of 1789
with both Houses were no longer by 1797 adequate to
contain the expanding printing needs of the government. The last years in Philadelphia saw more business
every quarter go to other shops than Fenno's and Ross's.
John Fenno died in September, '98. His son carried on,
John Ward Fenno, under his own imprint. The names
of Way and Groff of 27 Arch street—they, too, will follow the government to Washington—invade the official
preserve. They appear on a minor Senate committee
report,[70] on a House document of the greatest importance,[71] on Pickering's instructions to the XYZ min-
isters (in five hundred copies for the use of the Senate,[72]
and it must have been also, in so large a printing, for
general circulation), on a long, fifty-five-page House
document on impressment of seamen,[73] and on a number of others. J. Oswald in Second street does several
jobs for the House in '98; [74] Charles Cist published the
Post Office law and regulations, a book of a hundred
and more pages.

Thus by the end of the ten years in Philadelphia the
volume of governmental printing, expanded because
of the French War, had come into the stature of a big
and busy business. Philadelphia, fortunately, was a large
city, with plenty of printers to do the work. And the
government that had grown out of the "Child of fortune" Washington expected "to be fostered by some and

buffeted by others" had become the vested manager of a nation's affairs. It had "worked its way good."

Underneath every revolution in political structure has lain that administrative substructure of the working government which, while new interests seize the policy-making areas, remains unaffected, goes right on doing its daily task. It is the bureaucratic continuum of management. Bureaucracy creates an impermeable membrane within a government, so tough that almost nothing can puncture it. That had happened, by 1800, in America. So many areas of activity had been absorbed into the orbit of the Federal structure that never again would a failure in vitality threaten the existence of a Federal nexus. Never again, after One had arisen where there had formerly been Many, would the Many take back the functions they had formerly discharged.

Historically, it is correct in this country to believe the national constitution created the states, rather than was created by them. Historically, it is correct also to believe that the national government grew by governing, and by governing effectively.

All was not perfect in 1800. Printing arrangements, in their hurry too frequently haphazard, were not yet so stabilized in routine as to fulfill all the needs of the government for publishing, for proclaiming, for informing the people of the law. John Adams—in no very happy frame of mind as he left Philadelphia—proposed a change. "The President," said the President, "must issue proclamations, articles of war, articles of the navy, and must make appointments in the army, navy, revenue, and other branches of public service; and these ought all to be announced by authority in some acknowledged

gazette. The laws ought to be published in the same. . . .
It is certain that the present desultory manner of publishing the laws, acts of the President, and proceedings
of the Executive departments, is infinitely disgraceful to
the government and nation, and in all events must be
altered." [75]

It would be a hundred and thirty-six years before
Adams' complaints would be redressed by the founding
in 1936 of the *Federal Register*. But "infinitely disgraceful?"—the glum President was too harsh in 1800. That
very spring, he signed an Act of Congress erecting land
offices in Cincinnati, Chillicothe, Marietta, Steubenville,
dividing the townships west of Muskingum—the fresh
Western names fell with a strange sound at Sixth and
Chestnut streets in Philadelphia. The federal government over which Adams presided reached far into the
Western prairies, north to the mountain wilderness of
Maine, clear south to the swampy St. Mary's, and it
reached with effective power. Rebellion had been put
down in Pennsylvania, the Indian nations had been
defeated by the Federal Army at Fallen Timbers by the
rapids of the Maumee, out in what Randolph of Ro-
anoke would call "those geographical *expressions* beyond the Alleghenies," treaties had been made, a war
had been fought and won on the sea. And the free principles which the rugged Yankee president had long embraced were still the hallmark of the government,
stamped by its seal on every document.

While the bookbinder George Hyde packed up the
government's papers in chests, took them down to the
foot of Arch street to load on board the sloop *Unity*,
Captain Stiles, to be transported by river, bay, ocean,

bay, and river to the new Federal City on Potomac shores,[76] John Adams might have counted the gains instead of the unfilled promises of ten years.

And though we have not mentioned the big words of freedom in the government documents, they were there. President Adams might have considered that his was, after all, "this new man, this American's" government, which he had helped form; that government which, he deeply believed, more than any other political institution human beings had created in the long history of things hoped for and done, had approached closest to the rights of men in nature.

Of all people, John Adams might have acknowledged that his government had, for ten years, in the eloquent language of his former friend Alexander Hamilton, written the law of those unalienable rights, "as with a sunbeam."

3

Annuit Coeptis

ENTIRELY IN THE SPIRIT OF FAIR PLAY (AND I CLAIM SOME merit for that) I warned you at the beginning of this series that government documents are stiff, graceless things, scarcely the happiest subject for spirited discourse among polite people. Now, I am afraid, you are about to see how serious that warning was. For we have reached the point in our analysis where we descend— as the government moves in 1800 to the few half-finished buildings and sticky swamps called roads in the new Federal City on the Potomac—we descend from the taxonomy of the great charters and all the "firsts" of the 1780's, from the physiology of the Federalist administrations of the 1790's which converted the designs of the new constitution into action programs, we descend down to an essay in cytology—"the scientific investigation," said my college textbook many years ago, "of the constituent parts and functions of cells."

Cells are such tiny things, and there are such a lot of them, that we ask about each one only how well it operates individually in the economy of the whole body. Greely listed (including the *American State Papers* reprints, many of which were not published documents, though he sometimes considered them as such) above five thousand items of Congressional issue for the period 1789–1817, and he knew this to be incomplete—it was limited to Congress' publications only, and not even all of those. For the years in Washington 1801–17 there is still much to be discovered.

Some of the cells have a particular significance of their own. The administrations of Jefferson and Madison were full of vivid episodes, which made abundant records. The other day I had the good fortune of going through, in the collection of Mrs. Joseph Carson, a box of government imprints of the period 1800–16, which were preserved, happily, in their original pamphlet form, not bound up with others in dull smothering volumes. The art and architecture of a nation was in them, Hoban, Latrobe, Thornton; and science and invention, the far reaches west of the Louisiana purchase, Florida newly acquired, and all the vivid principles of Jefferson's original philosophy. They were worthy books; they deserved to be prized.

Some of them are excessively rare, and some raise unsolved problems disturbing or teasing. I have yet to discover what was the first government document printed in Washington, D.C. It was not, incidentally, the Ohio Land Sale report, prepared by Delegate William Henry Harrison and exhibited at The Clements Library in 1953 as printed in Washington. This important document had come from a Philadelphia press before the move. The Clements exhibit label should have read: "[Philadelphia, William Ross, printer.]" And apart from which was the *first* document printed by order in Washington, it is very hard indeed to locate *any* of the official printings of the year 1800–01, after the move. Collectors have never tried to, so far as I can learn. And bibliographers have not helped them.

It is curious. Washington was the first national city in Western history; after Philadelphia it was the second modern city to be planned before it was built. And it has been a continuing cultural excitement to our people for a century and a half. But its history has never been competently written. Errors and gossip have been repeated in book after book, until one despairs of finding the real events underneath. Washington local history is much worse even than the literature of Philadelphia history, which is saying quite a lot. And bibliographers of Washington printing have scarcely done better. All the bibliographers seem eager to tell us that six of the early printers became mayors of Washington, which indeed they did: Daniel Rapine, Roger Chew Weightman, Joseph Gales, Peter Force, W. W. Seaton, and John T. Towers. But even bibliographers should know that a printer is as likely to go to politics from failure as from success. What did they print, for whom, and for how much?

The late A. P. C. Griffin, Chief Bibliographer of The Library of Congress, read and published a study in 1900 which he called "Issues of the District of Columbia Press in 1800–01–02." [1] In it he described with some care the private issues of the first printers to locate in Georgetown, Alexandria, and the new city too. But the public printing—that government work which, after all, the printers went to Washington to do, and which, one thinks, would be the only important reason for studying issues of the District of Columbia press at all—he dis-

missed with the casual observation, "The printing of
public documents of course formed a large part of the
productions of the press during this period. I have not
attempted to mention them all, and note the following
as being of special interest:" [2] and then he listed Charles
Goldsborough's Naval List of 1800, no printer given,
which would be of the most vital interest to us because
it is an 1800 issue if it were a public document, but it
is not; the *Rules and Articles for the Better Government of the Troops,* which was that old 1775 work revised, now printed by William Duane's new Apollo
Press in 1801 or 1802 at no government order but as a
private venture; and finally the *Message from the President* of 15 December, 1802, printed by Duane, indis-
putably a Senate document—but one, you will notice,
issued fully two years and some months after the government had reached the city. Griffin's concern for public
documents was as primitive, as unawakened, apparently,
as Joseph Sabin's or Charles Evans'.

Bibliographers have missed a big story here. The
movement of printers to Washington in 1800 was an
important episode in the annals of the printing craft
in America. What machinery they took, where they
found workmen, where they bought type and paper, how
they conducted their business and what it consisted of,
all present a lively picture of professional trade and
practices at the commencement of a great century. The
years from the beginning in that midsummer of 1800
to the fire in August, 1814, form a period that should
be better known. It begins with the scenes of migration,
it ends with the equally creative scenes of rebuilding
the city.

Eight or nine printers moved to Washington with the government.³ William Alexander Rind was set up by September 25, 1800, in Georgetown. Samuel Harrison Smith, aged twenty-eight, Secretary of the American Philosophical Society, with his Philadelphia bride of a few days, began his *National Intelligencer* on October 31. Way and Groff from Philadelphia found a place on the pasture vaguely called North E street, "near the General Post Office," that year. Like Duane, they published the *Rules and Articles for the Troops* as their first imprint, and let us particularly notice that they issued the *Journal of the Senate,* Sixth Congress, 2nd Session, which began November 7, 1800, ended March 3, 1801. Let us particularly notice this, because if they printed the journals for Mr. Otis in weekly half-sheets, then the first week's delivered sheets may have been that first government imprint in the new capital city which I have been looking for.

William Ross, the House printer, also came down to the new capital from Philadelphia, but I think he lasted only a short while. I cannot find how long. Most important of the printers of the first year was another Philadelphia migrant, Rapine Conrad and Co., all arranged and ready to print when Congress met. Daniel Rapine had brought with him the brothers Michael and John Conrad, bookbinders, and a stock of books and stationery for sale. This partnership lasted till 1806, when the Conrads left, and Rapine took in Jonathan Eliot, whose public career just then began. Joseph Gales senior with his fourteen-year-old son, meanwhile, had left Philadelphia for Raleigh, North Carolina, and would not come to Washington till the year 1807, to join Samuel

Harrison Smith, later (1810) to take over the *National Intelligencer*. William Duane, who once he got started quickly became the major printer for the Senate, did not get his Apollo Press started in Washington till late in 1801, a whole year after the government's move. His tardy arrival is one factor which makes the imprints for the first year, 1800–01, so difficult to identify and describe. They could not have been Duane imprints, at least not Duane *Washington* imprints.

Now it gravely endangered the bureaucratic procedures Clerk Beckley and Secretary Otis had developed in Philadelphia to move from a large and flourishing city to a village with no printing trade, no paper mill within forty miles, no large population to support a bookstore, no wholesalers to furnish supplies. Even with all the able clerks had accomplished before the move in 1800, laws were not widely enough distributed, the people were not well enough informed of their government's doings. Too often the Senate could not find a copy of its own printed *Journal*. And the move in 1800 coincided with another risk—the shift in philosophy of government from Federalist to Republican, from Alexander Hamilton to Thomas Jefferson.

Federalists had been big-government men, mercantilists and physiocrats, social planners. The general government, said General Hamilton, must "not only have a strong soul, but *strong organs* by which that soul is to operate." Federalists favored a permanent, well-paid civil service. "No government costs so much as a bad one," Hamilton observed. Republicans, to the alarm of the hard-working bureaucrats, were anti-government men. Mr. Jefferson wanted frequent rotation of office holders. He recommended, as what he termed "a wise and necessary precaution against the degeneracy of the public servants," that government workers be paid at a level of "drudgery and subsistence only." Not till Quincy Adams in the 1820's attacked "the niggardly theories of Mr. Jefferson" would the concept of government as leader and servant of the people begin to return to something like Hamilton's concept: "majestic, efficient, and operative of great things." [4]

Devoted public servants, reasonably enough, did not relish being described as tending toward degeneracy, nor being paid drudgery and subsistence only. They did not like the scurrilous party songs:

> Since JEFFERSON now, is our Leader and Chief
> And Placemen compell'd to turn o'er a new leaf . . .

It was genuinely distressing to such a conscientious person as Otis to be called a placeman, to have Republicans from his own Massachusetts speak of the inevitable corruption in public officeholders, their lust for power (as if he had any), their untrustworthiness. Jeffersonians, the Federalists thought, seemed determined to elevate distrust to a political principle. And unquestionably it was true that the new philosophy, "whatever government is best, which governs least," impeded bureaucratic reform in the years 1800–16. The needed expansion in printing budgets, the desirable enlargement of editions and increase of things printed could not come under a Jeffersonian economy, the tendency of which was to reduce the functional costs of government.

After the fire of 1814, and particularly in the 1820's when the Fiftieth Anniversary celebrations of successive events of the Revolution began, a wave of historical curiosity would sweep the country, aided and abetted by government-sponsored publications. In this later era, people would suddenly want to know every detail of their government's past. Wait's *State Papers* appeared, and Eliot's *Debates,* and Madison's *Notes,* the second reprint (that by Way and Gideon) of the Continental Congress *Journals,* and the first edition of the *Secret Journals;* the great series of *American State Papers* under the direction of both houses, Jared Sparks's *Diplomatic Correspondence of the American Revolution,* the magnificently conceived but truncated *American Archives* of Peter Force. The Senate ordered its *Executive Journals* made public. Even the Supreme Court, though it still published nothing, finally appointed an official reporter. When all this historical searching began, in the time of the second Adams and Jackson, it was already too late to recover much that had been destroyed. Not all the loss had been caused by the British fire in the library. Some must be charged to the frugality of the administrations which printed too little, distributed it uneconomically, and hired too few office workers.

Until very recent times in its history, Washington has ever been a poor town for businessmen to make a living in. It certainly was at the beginning. Proprietors of print shops frequently failed, and their printers, in an almost vain hope of security, very early organized. The first call for journeymen to form an association was November 2, 1807. In January, 1815, with the war not yet over, the Columbia Typographical Society became a permanent reality. Printing contracts had to be drawn with a higher labor cost factor as the union emerged, and as competition stabilized among a shrinking group of proprietors. This was an element in government publishing.

But so was a more basic factor an element, the common denominator of all American history, the irresistible groundswell of growth. The purity of Jeffersonian theory was soon modified in practice, and the years 1800–16 saw the inevitable enlargement of government as the nation that bought Louisiana suddenly by the squeaking of a quill spanned a continent, as the nation dedicated to aloofness from European broils abruptly, surprisingly, took a belated and expensive part in the World War raging in 1812–15. Practice defeated theory, and the government, on an austere functional budget, enlarged every year in substantive expenditures.

These first years in Washington, before the watershed time of 1816, these years when the bureaucracy had to re-form itself and manage great things in a forest village waiting to grow up around it, represented a new start after Philadelphia. And as before, we turn to the papers of the United States Senate for such a view as the records allow us into how the people were served with news of their country's laws.

On September 19, 1814, a third session of the Thirteenth Congress assembled, meeting in dismal makeshift quarters. It was less than a month since Ross and Cockburn had set their tar barrels, rockets, broken chairs, and heaps of books from Congress' library a'burning. The White House was in ruins, so were all the government buildings except the Patent Office (which the courage of Dr. Thornton had saved: "Are you Brit-

ish soldiers or are you barbarians?" he had cried from
the porch of his Parthenon), so were various private
homes, the print shop of the *National Intelligencer,* and
of course the capitol building itself. That handsome
pair of lower rooms in the North Wing, 24 by 36 feet
each, 22 feet high, in which Samuel Allyne Otis had
proudly, skillfully discharged his duties as Secretary of
the Senate, was a shambles.

Even worse, for the Senators, their Secretary himself
was gone. Four days after adjournment the previous
April, Mr. Otis, at the age of seventy-four, had suddenly died. For twenty-five years he had administered
the business of the Senate, ever since the very first days
of the First Congress. Perhaps it was a happiness that
he was spared the spectacle of British destruction in
Washington City. His cherished routines, the even
tenor of his efficient ways, would have been desperately
disturbed. His death was the end of an era in American
bureaucracy.

To succeed him, making the first break in the continuous administrative history of their house, the Senators chose a lame-duck member just defeated in election, Charles Cutts of New Hampshire. Senator Cutts
found Otis' papers in perfect order, marvelously preserved from the fire. He took over the duties of the Secretary, and discharged them well enough. But it was
Otis who had set the pattern, shaped the office, established the procedures and made them work. And it is
the file Otis kept of the housekeeping records of the
Senate, surviving in the National Archives today, that
gives us such insight as we have into the printing activi-

ties of the government during its first years in Washington.

It is useless to say Gilbert Stuart's portrait of Samuel Allyne Otis makes him look aristocratic. Stuart's portrait of any gentleman made him look pink and white and aristocratic. Otis had the high forehead and long thin nose Stuart did so well; he wore his own gray hair, combed back over what even the elegant painter of the elegant must have thought were unnecessarily large ears. His manners were gallant and gracious, his patience inexhaustible. He had been born the tenth of thirteen children. His sister was the brilliant Mercy Otis Warren, that avid and tireless female historan; his eldest brother was the patriot James Otis, and Samuel Allyne Otis had been guardian of the famous orator during the long years he lived in his piteous half-world of insanity.

The Secretary's life had been various. In his time of prosperity and prominence during the Revolutionary War his first wife had died, leaving five motherless children. Soon afterwards, postwar inflation and the debts of another brother had plunged him into bankruptcy. His second marriage brought his children a guide, and himself some peace; appointment as Secretary of the Senate in 1789 gave him security and a place, tiny but worthy, in the big world of affairs.

Rarely was a man, for his talents, more agreeably situated. Mr. Otis was businesslike; he knew all the tricks of tradesmen, for he had been one. Still, he dined with the Adamses, the Grays, the Gerrys, the Warrens, he was at home in any society, and if his instincts were those of the fine Federalist world of Boston commerce, he could nevertheless deal efficiently even with the rough new elements of Mr. Jefferson's party. His son's partisan enthusiasms, when Harrison Gray Otis, too, came first to Philadelphia, then to Washington as a Federalist Congressman, might have embarrassed a less urbane father. Blandly, Mr. Otis ignored the issues of party, and wrote President Jefferson urging his son's merits, begging the new President in 1801 to continue the young man in the midnight appointment Adams had conferred upon him, ". . . in doing which you will oblige an affectionate father," the Secretary declared.[5] Of course Mr. Jefferson did not; but the Senators, all through the Republican election and victory which Federalists called "The Great Subversion," continued the father as their administrative official. Not even the rowdiest of the Republicans thought of dropping him, though Hamiltonians warned Mr. Otis they would. The Secretary went right on, a curious relic of former days, able and surefooted in the loose shale of political slopes.

He reached Washington before the Senators; he set busily to work. After the first year of settlement was over, the printer he had to deal most with was William Duane, the same Duane he had seen haled to the bar of the Senate for contempt and "high breach of the privileges of this house" back in Philadelphia.

"Having opened a Store for the Supply of the public Offices with every species of Stationary, and established a Printing office adequate to the execution of any kind or quantity of work," Duane wrote Mr. Otis on November 7, 1801, "I take the liberty of intimating that I shall be obliged by your commands in either of those branches when you may have occasion to obtain stationary, or

printing for the Senate of the United States." [6] Duane
was too closely connected with Jefferson and the new
party to go unrewarded. Three months later he submits
a bill for ten items he has printed for the Senate in
November and December, 1801, January 1802; [7] another quarter and he is asking, may he draw on Otis
for any part of his printing account, for he needs cash
to pay his workmen.[8]

Now Otis preferred that payments be regularly made
in the ordinary way, by the Treasury. This was not good
enough for Duane, who girded himself in all his political influence and went over to the Treasury in person,
where he was permitted to find out that Secretary Otis
had an unexpended surplus in the contingent fund of
the Senate. He promptly wrote again, explaining his
bill was about $2,000, asking Mr. Otis please to pay him
at once $1,500. Or if not that, then how about a thou-
sand? [9]

Otis was patient. He was less patient, when Duane
tried to pass the blame for late work. The bill for or-
ganizing courts in Tennessee he had sent to the printer
Daniel Rapine two days ago in the evening, he said.
Rapine told Otis at once it had not come to him at that
time, indeed not till this very morning.[10] Rapine was
easier to deal with. So was Wells, the binder.[11] By and
by Duane acquired assistants, who managed things better. Young William Kean from his shop is writing the
Secretary by January, 1804. He appears to be more
businesslike, more amenable: [12]

The Bill for the erection of Louisiana into two separate
territories are all worked off, and are now folding and stitching [he writes], and shall be sent up to your office immedi-

ately after they are finished—If you think it necessary I shall set the printers to work have [*sic*] you a second edition stricken off agreeably to your alterations.

Even Duane himself, as problems arise that factional preferment cannot solve, makes an effort. He has received copy so late today he cannot deliver the document early tomorrow, he explains, but if Mr. Otis will read the proof he sends and return it with the messenger, "the business will be much expedited." [13]

Unquestionably, Duane was difficult, and not just to Federalists. Republican Senators, however biased in the printer's favor, still had to have the work of the Senate done. One Republican raised a sharp objection—an objection of a sort Otis had never met with in ten years of Philadelphia and New York printing. "Sir," Senator John Breckenridge, chairman of the vital committee on the Louisiana Purchase, demanded of the Secretary, "Under whose direction was it, that, the Words 'And be it further enacted that' were inserted at the Beginning of every Section of the Louis.ª Territory Bill. Such liberty was improperly assumed, & they must be stricken out before the copies are delivered to the Members." Otis was genuinely embarrassed. "The above words were inserted by the printer in deviation from the copy," he responded, "as I found by inspection thereof." And he added, "Had the printer followed copy no ground of censure would have occurred." [14]

But difficult or not, Duane was receiving the lion's share of the Senate business. His bills for "printing, folding, & stitching" list all the items he handled by name, and the number of copies he issued. For the Eighth Congress, first session, his account in March,

1804, was $4,655.50. For 1805 it was $2,265; for 1806, $2,458.50.[15] Otis was careful to keep him to contract. No such agreeable understanding ever existed with the Democratic printer of the Apollo Press as the Secretary had enjoyed in Philadelphia with the elder John Fenno.

The House, whose Clerk John Beckley was a Virginian, dealt mostly with A. and G. Way, though sometimes also with Duane, and when this latter relationship occurred, it was an easy thing for both men, for Clerk Beckley was as Republican as Secretary Otis was Federalist. Beckley developed his House office, with clear purpose, along completely different lines from those Otis followed in the Senate. While Otis withdrew himself and his job from the political arena, Beckley plunged all his energies and official resources into the very midst of it. As Clerk, he had very few of those housekeeping skills that make the investigator today so grateful to the Senate Secretary. He should have had; behind him lay ten years of clerkly experience in a state legislature.

Neither Otis nor Beckley was deemed worthy of inclusion in the *Dictionary of American Biography*. They received brief notices in Appleton long ago. Beckley deserves more. Recently, Professor Philip Marsh has described him as "mystery man of the early Jeffersonians," and "the undercover political strategist of his time," which I think extravagant phrases suggesting a melodrama that was not actually there. Beckley is more properly to be thought a player of minor political games, a moderately successful factional plotter. Unquestionably, he was well known to Jefferson, Madison, Gallatin, Duane; unquestionably, he regarded himself, in the fashion of partisans, as an "enemy" of Hamilton, John Adams, Pickering, Mr. Otis, all the Federalists.

John James Beckley was born in Louisa County, Virginia, in 1757, the son of an English knight and a Virginia lady. He was taken to England as a child, sent to school at Eton—surprising preparation for a Jeffersonian factionalist. Then after his father's death in 1771 he was brought back to America, studied at William and Mary, was one of the original members of the Phi Beta Kappa Society there. He served briefly in the Virginia militia in the Revolutionary War, but most of the time from 1776 to 1785 he was assistant clerk or clerk to the House of Delegates, and to the Virginia Senate. He went clear to Philadelphia in 1787, expecting to be chosen secretary of the Federal Convention, but he lost out to William Jackson. He was, however, mayor of Richmond, and secretary to the Virginia Ratification Convention of 1788.

The House of Representatives of the new government elected him Clerk at the beginning, April, 1789. He held this position till May 15, 1797, when by the vote of a Federalist majority of one he was ousted. He spent three and a half years in political writing and a malicious sort of gossipy campaigning. After Jefferson's election, he was once again chosen Clerk by the now Republican House, on December 7, 1801, and kept the job until his death in April, 1807.

Beckley was a close friend of Freneau and of Benjamin Franklin Bache, Duane's predecessor as editor of the *Aurora*. Once he stopped a fist fight between Bache and young John Ward Fenno. It was Beckley who made public Hamilton's sordid affair with Mrs. Reynolds, and precipitated that crisis. He supplied endless gossip about Federalists, even rumors about Washington and Adams, to Jefferson and Madison; Monroe described him as a close friend.

On his return to his clerkship, Beckley was also created librarian to Congress (Jan. 26-29, 1802), and given care of "the accumulated books and maps" of the members. He was not much concerned to do a good job with this. Indeed, throughout his years as Clerk, Beckley used his position more for political than for administrative purposes. He should have had Duane for his printing. He would have had less trouble with the partisan editor.[16]

Mr. Otis had more than his share of trouble. To Duane, as the Ninth Congress began, the Secretary sent a firm notice: "I requested your clerk here to state to you that I should continue the printing ordered by the Senate US in your office provided it be done on the same terms as that for the H of R US is effected. I am by him led to understand that you agree to that proposition. It would however give more satisfaction to have you explicit on the subject." [17]

Not all of Duane's charges pleased the careful Secretary. He objected once to how much engrossers were being paid. As it happened, this particular matter was not an issue on which Duane was guilty either of carelessness or of partisan exploitation of his government connections. He simply had to pay the going rates. He explained his difficulties in a letter that gives us some insight into printing-house wages in the year 1806. For the urgent Senate work of engrossing acts, he said, three of his men worked almost entirely at night. Two of them had just finished thirty-two hours, equal to five days and two hours each, at $6.00 per day. The third had completed twenty-four hours, or the equivalent of four days. He pointed out that services at night in every government department were ordinarily paid double the compensation for day work. He was actually saving the Senate money on this, for he was giving only time-and-a-half. Four dollars a day, he added, was a good and reasonable pay for engrossers.[18] And as for printing at the rates the House of Representatives secured from the printers, Mr. Otis must remember that there were only thirty-four Senators (1806), but one hundred forty-two representatives, and so many more copies, as well as so much bulkier journals, made the House per-unit printing cost lower.[19]

By the spring of 1807, Duane himself was not dealing with Otis any longer. He was turning Senate matters over to his clerk or assistant, young Roger Chew Weightman, and this was the beginning of a much different relationship between Secretary and printer. In seven years of close association, Mr. Otis never learned to spell Weightman's name correctly (he always wrote it Wightman; apparently that was how it was pronounced), but he did learn to rely on him, and to expect good and speedy performance of the Senate's business from the enterprising artisan.

Enterprising, young Weightman certainly was. While still Duane's clerk, he wrote Otis a persuasive plea for the contract to bind up three hundred copies of the *Acts* for Congress' library, a responsibility Otis by statute had been charged with.[20] And only two months later, at the end of May, 1807, he informed the Secretary, who was then home in Boston during the long recess, that he had bought out William Duane—purchased "the whole of his establishment in this city with the expectation of succeeding to his business." [21] The Apollo Press was ended. Before Otis returned to Washington that October, Duane had wound up his affairs in the capital and gone back to his newspaper in Philadelphia, and to subsequent lively adventures far removed from the sphere in which Mr. Otis lived.

Now Roger Chew Weightman was a youth only twenty years and four months old when he somehow raised the money to buy out William Duane's print shop at Pennsylvania avenue and Sixth street in the capital, and take over all his custom. He had no political influence to bludgeon the Secretary with. He was only a nervy youngster on the make, just the sort of person Otis could handle with ease. And his only sure way to success lay in prompt and accurate execution of such commissions as he could get. He was really dependent on the Senate printing contract. Just at this moment, with the new Tenth Congress not yet formed, a new letting of that contract was due. "Mr. D has signified to me that he will relinquish all claims to the business of the Senate in my favor," the boy wrote hopefully to Otis in Boston. "The object therefore of the present application is to ascertain whether you would be perfectly satisfied that I should, instead of Mr Duane, become printer, stationer and binder to the Senate. I bought the establishment under the impression that I should succeed to the whole of the business, and under this impression I have taken the liberty of addressing you." [22]

For all that his mother was a Germantown Chew, the new young printer was a native of the District. He had been born in Alexandria. His father for a while lived in Philadelphia, then moved to Washington when the government came. At fourteen, in 1801, young Roger had been apprenticed to Way and Groff. By the beginning of the year 1805 [23] he had moved to Duane.[24] He was not one of your political immigrants, he belonged here. The printer Jonathan Eliot recommended him to Otis, and Vice President Clinton too thought he would do for the Senate business. "I expect to get the contract for supplying the House of Reps. with stationery, and will in consequence be able to furnish the Senate on the most reasonable terms," Weightman explained to Otis. "The printing I propose to execute at the price it was done at the last two sessions. The whole of the business shall be done on such reasonable terms as to leave no blame with you. . . . You will be good enough, Sir, to give this as early an answer as possible, and to state explicitly what I have to expect." [25]

Now Mr. Otis had often seen the Weightman youngster standing politely by his desk as William Duane's messenger, with proof sheets in his hand. To think of him as the proprietary printer on his own responsibility, at so early an age, was something of a wrench. It was also an opportunity to get the upper hand at once. From Boston, Mr. Otis answered, with that critical reserve experienced oldsters can use so adroitly to dampen the enthusiasm and if possible destroy the pleasures of ambitious youths. Some senators had complained of the printing in the past, he observed. Some had even wondered why they should not employ the same printer as the House. "However," he added, almost grudgingly, "when the Senate come together, if they approve of your executing the business, I have no objection." [26]

The Weightman youngster succeeded very well. His bills were as large as Duane's,[27] he hired plenty of printers—a man named James W. Bryson was his clerk or foreman—he was even brash enough to scold Mr. Otis when that gentleman had chided him. The Senate messengers do not deliver corrected proofs promptly, he charged, more than once. They neglect their work, they cause confusion, delays, and expense by dawdling.[28] He asked for estimates of the amount of Senate printing in advance so he could buy enough paper on his trips to Philadelphia.[29] And against Mr. Otis' criticisms he defended himself with spirit: [30]

> The petitions & memorials will make from 160 to 200 pages—and it is obvious that a pamphlet of such a size cannot be printed in 4 or 5 days. I have had 8 or 10 hands at work ever since they have been received—and with all the exertion I have been able to make I cannot possibly have them ready for delivery before Monday morning. This I regret, but it is unavoidable—and I [am] sure when you see the size of the pamphlet you will be satisfied that it is impossible to have it done sooner.

Happily for the historian of printing, the busy boy with his ten and more workers listed his charges for paper, for engrossing, for folding and stitching separately from his charges for composition and impressing. Thus in December, 1809, the *Message of the President* cost the Senate $260 to print in five hundred copies on thirteen 8vo half sheets; it cost $20.60 to fold and stitch. "Mr. Giles' Motion," 250 copies, on one quarter-sheet

8vo, cost $7.00 to print, 60 cents to fold. And so on. Two parchments, for engrossing headings of acts, were billed at $2.25 each. There are many of these quarterly bills and accounts surviving.[31]

Daily dealing with Mr. Otis by and by relieved Weightman of all the youthful diffidence he at first felt toward a man thirty-seven years his senior. Once, when the appropriations bill was long delayed in passing and Otis had not the money to pay the printing bills, Weightman, much as he had seen Mr. Duane do, went over the Senate's head and called upon the Secretary of the Treasury himself. He needed at least a thousand dollars on his account, he explained, to pay his men and to purchase supplies in Philadelphia. Secretary Gallatin, smoking his eternal cigar, observed in his quaint thick foreign accent that it was entirely unimportant which fund the money came from. Why not have Otis take a thousand dollars out of the fund for the Senators' salaries, pay the printer, later replace the withdrawal by a requisition on his contingent fund when the appropriations had passed? [32] The scrupulous Otis was horrified, and of course did no such thing. Neither did he do what Patrick Magruder, Beckley's successor as Clerk of the House, did—give his personal note to his printer to ensure payment of the printing contract.[33] Weightman had to wait for his money. The same delay occurred the next year; [34] collecting from the government was a continual vexation to an employer with workmen to pay.

It was a particularly hard problem in those years when Congress adjourned early in the spring, not to commence again till November. Otis would be in Boston. The only printing would be left-over jobs or the few continuing items. One such continuing item in 1811 was the survey of coasts and harbors Jefferson had recommended and Congress had approved back in 1807. This is the very beginning of the Coast and Geodetic Survey, which for a variety of reasons characteristic of governments would not get really started for another twenty-five years.[35] In 1811 Ferdinand Rudolph Hassler, who had been chosen for the work, prepared a report, with plates. Late in June, Weightman wrote to Secretary Otis up in Boston that the plates (which had been made at his order in another city) had long been delayed, and when finally shipped took a month in transit. The report had still to be printed before Professor Hassler's imminent departure for Europe: Weightman had no money. His account was about $450. Could he please have that sum? "Our only dependence for a summer's support is entirely on little pickings of this sort. We are in fact at this season of the year always paying and but seldom receiving." [36]

The long walk from Sixth and Pennsylvania up and down Capitol Hill was a nuisance, especially when pressure was hard and messengers unreliable. Sometimes Weightman would go up himself during evening sessions, and send a note in by a page to the Secretary at his desk in the well of the Senate. "I have stepped up here with a view of getting the remainder of the documents . . . which the compositor is now waiting for. . . ." [37]

When Otis objected to printing costs, Weightman was firm with him, and sometimes, after the fashion of the young, didactic. I hope it amused the mannerly old

Boston Federalist to have the youthful printer instruct
him in bookbinding, an art he had surely known about
long before Weightman's birth: "The trouble of binding books—and the expense is not lessened because they
are *thin* books," the printer scrawled. "If however this
were the case—the extra trouble of lettering on the side
would fully counterbalance the absence of *thickness*." [38]
On another occasion, Otis complained of the amount
of paper used in the *Journal*, and wondered why it
could not be set solid, as the House *Journal* was. Did
not Mr. Weightman's conscience bother him? Mr.
Weightman, who was now, at twenty-five, first lieutenant
of the Washington Light Horse, ready for action in Mr.
Madison's War, answered with asperity that his conscience had nothing to do with the spacing of the lines.
"I leave that to those who first established the form. I
simply followed the track that was marked out, when I
became printer to the Senate." The House *Journal* was
set solid because it was bulky, the Senate *Journal* leaded
because it was much scantier. His workmen were actually obliged to extend the Senate *Journal* "as otherwise
it would often happen that a fortnight would elapse
before there would be matter enough to make a single
half sheet. As it is, a week's proceedings are sometimes
found insufficient for that purpose." [39]

Financial success, as well as the militia commission,
brought Weightman self-assurance. After 1811, he was
buying the properties around him on Sixth street, Pennsylvania, and C, planning fine buildings with apart-
ments for rent; "the Weightman buildings," they would
be called. In 1812, he was chosen a member of City
Council. He was busy, and prominent. Experienced

oldsters never seem to sense just when youngsters grow
up. The time came when Mr. Otis' criticisms of the
printing would strike the militia officer and Councilman
as entirely unnecessary, sometimes merely aged petulance. No one can be as short with aged petulance as a
nervy young man on the make, who has made it. Your
corrections have come in this night after the sheets are
all worked off, he wrote Mr. Otis brusquely in one note.
The title is not wrong, as you have thought; it corre-
sponds exactly to the words of the President in his
message.[40]

Another time, Otis raised his order for the report of
the Committee on Ways and Means he had sent down
earlier in the day, by thirty copies. One form had
already been taken off the press, Weightman answered
by messenger, but he would order it put back, and order
thirty more copies drawn. He was always disposed to
give the Senators what they wished.[41] Actually, this was
youthful petulance. Just to get the upper hand over
Mr. Otis in a busy moment during the war, Weightman
had told a small falsehood. The form, far from being
impressed and taken off, had not even been locked up
yet, and Otis, by one of those improbable accidents
which with tedious regularity favor the virtuous, caught
the young man out in his indiscretion. If the form is
off and some sheets have already been impressed, he
wrote back by messenger, send them on up here right
away. And Weightman had to retreat. He should have
been contrite, but of course he was not. Growing up
does not happen all at once. In a note the next day he
took refuge in defense, as a young man will: "I have
not had the Report in my possession *two days—*" he

declared. "Every exertion has been made to get it to the Senate by 2 o'clock tomorrow." [42]

Mr. Otis could not have been surprised. He certainly knew all a Boston Otis needed to know about the difference, in conduct and address, between a gentleman born and a successful apprentice rising in the world's way to wealth.

Yet there was much that was admirable in the vigorous young printer. Weightman had educated himself, he was good at his trade and good at managing men, he surrounded himself with a group of young inquirers after truth in a sort of regular study club quite like the Juntos Addison or Franklin had started, his public activities in militia and Common Council made him look a likely, coming leader in citizens' affairs. He was also a merchant. And in this Mr. Otis understood him, for getting and spending was ever the true vocation of a Boston gentleman born.

As private merchant, Weightman sold "yarns, plaid shirtings, chambrays, sattenettes, chocolate, sugar, and nails" to the custom.[43] As public merchant—stationer to the Congress officially—he sold to Mr. Otis for the Senators a variety of supplies: paper of all kinds, pens, pencils, Dutch wax, oil pots, desk sanders, sand strainers, red wafers, Japanned tin wafer boxes, corn brooms, hickory brooms, sail needles, small Wedgewood ink pots, black lead, pen knives, india rubbers, balls of twine, hand quills, long rules and round rules, gums, pitchers, glass tumblers, large hand "lanthorns," and, to set our imaginations going astray about the Senators, "one dozen diaper napkins." [44] In one three-months' period his stationery bill was $380.86.[45] When the war

came in 1812, paper was a scarce item difficult to procure, but he got the best to be had, and he smarted
under criticism. "If any person about the Senate expects
better than the best he must necessarily be disap-
pointed," he informed the Secretary.[46] Weightman made
his purchases mostly in Philadelphia, where he sent his
assistant or his brother to buy supplies. Many times in
his notes concerning the printing in hand he would add
a sentence to acquaint Otis with desk supplies he had
stocked for the members: pen knives, inkwells, a thousand pencils he himself had imported from Europe.[47]

From one of his wartime letters leaps the arresting
sentence, "there is no red tape in the United States."
By this he meant, of course, red tape. He had searched
all the stores in three cities—New York, Philadelphia,
and Baltimore: "there is not a dozen a piece to be had."
He ordered white tape manufactured, in order that
Congress might at least keep at work.[48]

When the Twelfth Congress sat far into midsummer
in 1812, and the War began, both houses had to print
so much more than usual that their moneys ran out.
Mr. Otis secured an additional $2,500 from his Sena-
tors.[49] The war steadily multiplied work and costs, and
finally budgets. By 1814, the contingent fund was $40,-
000 for the House (185 members), $10,000 for the Sen-
ate (36 members).[50] Of Otis' $10,000 a very large part
could be counted on each year to go to Weightman for
printing, engrossing, binding, and stationery. On this
as the nucleus of his business the young printer did
pretty well. He was scrupulous about following the
contract rules: he refused a request of the Secretary of

State, because it violated a practice Otis had established.[51] House printing was proportionately larger.

By the hard year 1812, Mr. Otis, somewhat irascible in his old age, fixed in his bureaucratic routines, found the quick pace of war a trial and confusion. There was such urgency about everything, particularly, it seemed, about everything the busy young Weightman was concerned with. "Is it too late this evening to expect any part of the copy?" Weightman would write on a hot Sunday night in July. "I shall be ready for it the moment it reaches me. . . . I am sanding the last two proofs at this moment—they will be forwarded to you in half an hour." [52] Weightman lived at a pace much faster than the old gentleman at his desk in the well of the Senate. But whenever the Secretary would turn in agitation from his energetic principal contractor to other printers, Gales and Seaton or the Ways, complaints would follow.[53] Weightman was unquestionably the best printer for Otis to use. They were used to each other. Even so, Weightman was sometimes slow with his work, and sometimes pressed too hard upon Otis with his demands. The Navy Register should have been ready sooner, Otis complained.[54] And the printer annoyed the Secretary by publishing some extracts from the *Journal* at Senator Leib's request directly, instead of through Otis.[55] The old man was eternally being assailed by the printer's call for more *Journal* copy to fill up half sheets.[56]

Perhaps the messengers were at fault. Weightman tactfully suggested it, when he asked that copy come in earlier each day. "For these last two evenings," he wrote, "I have not receive[d] the copy till between the hours

of 6 and 7, just as the hands were about to retire for the
day. As I am sensible that these delays are unknown to
Mʳ Otis, I have deemed it right to make it known. . . ." [57]
Or perhaps Weightman was just too busy. He was printing for the House, too, in 1813 and '14.[58] Frequently
he vexed Mr. Otis by pointing out the differences between the two bodies in their requirements, or men-
tioning directions Mr. Otis had given that were plainly
wrong: Does the joint resolution requiring 200 additional copies include acts as well as other documents?
he asks. He will keep his type standing till Otis answers.
The resolution seems to mean everything should be
printed in 200 copies more, but Mr. Otis has marked
only "50 copies" on his margins.[59]

Secretary Otis had no wish to discuss his mistakes.
Rather, he wanted to know why Weightman had numbered the pages wrong in the *Acts*. Because he wanted
the Senate printing to correspond with the Department
of State edition, Weightman answered, so both printings could be bound together by any who wished.[60]

As 1814 began, the young printer and the old Secretary were trapped in continual tiny misunderstandings,
and the young printer, with an access of maturity agreeable to contemplate at this distance, was handling the
tired Otis gently, as becomes a junior when an oldster
is failing. Clerk Magruder of the House disagrees with
you about that joint resolution, Weightman observed.
He has charged two hundred additional copies of everything including acts to his contingent fund. Otis' wishes
will be followed to the letter with the Senate charges,
but the printer cannot, as Otis has suggested, accept
the direction of the Secretary of State. "The Secretary

of State, it is believed," said the printer in 1814 in language which Mr. Otis himself might have written in 1789, "has no controul over the printing nor has he any thing to do with payment—This appertains to the Secretary of the Senate and Clerk of the House of Representatives."

And he added, in words too which the old Secretary would in a happier day have seconded, "I conceive that it is intended [by the joint resolution] to have the bills distributed with the other documents, that everybody may see and understand, the *beginning, progress,* and *termination* of every bill introduced to the notice of Congress." [61]

Soon, Attorney General Rush would edit the new edition of all the Laws of the United States, in five volumes. But meanwhile the old custom of the slip-law separates would continue, as it does to this day, and the printer himself was striving in the midst of Mr. Madison's War for the larger distribution, the better public information, which John Adams back in 1800 had demanded.

Indeed, the printer after seven years of direction and straightening from Mr. Otis, had himself become a conscientious servant in a new government tradition. The last communication that passed from Weightman to Mr. Secretary Otis was a hasty scrawl delivered by messenger just a few days before the old gentleman's death, near the adjournment of the session: "I sent you up this morning almost a cart load of printing—everything indeed except the Bill reported by Mr. Bibb, which is now on the press, and will not be printed before 3 or 4 o'clock. R. C. Weightman. Apl 6. 1814." [62]

In history, as I am sure is true in the mysterious pursuit of cytology as well, the examination of one group of cells must substitute for the scrutiny of all. History is imaginative reconstruction from fragments. I wish the intramural records of the Clerk of the House of Representatives relating to his printing had been preserved. I wish the correspondence files of Daniel Rapine and A. & G. Way and W. A. Davis and Joseph Gales and W. W. Seaton and all the others had survived. So far as I know, they did not. But it has been, I hope, possible, by the contemplation of the one cell, Secretary Otis at work in his administrative responsibility, to see what the problems were, and the procedures, of printing the government's public work.

Reconstruction followed, after the war, and numerous reforms, and numerous changes that were not reforms. Mr. George Watterston, Librarian of Congress, or as he was sometimes called, Librarian of the United States, moved into his rebuilt quarters. He had Rapine do his binding, Weightman supply his ink, Eliot print 11,100 spine labels and 11,100 bookplates at 50 cents a hundred, 48 large shelf labels at a dollar each. And he paid $972.37 to the binder Joseph Milligan to pack the books purchased from former President Jefferson and transport them from Monticello to the new Library rooms.

The reconstruction, however, is another story. Our tracing of the literary career of the United States Government as author, which began with the Bradfords issue of the continental *Association* in the fall of 1774, will end with this picture of the printing practices that had become routine in the growing Federal City by the time the official contractor who had grown up with that city, could himself urge upon the government such procedures as would enable everybody to "see and understand."

Our author is still in the early stages of his career, in 1814; and soon all the mechanics of his creative production will be re-examined and rearranged, not entirely, truth to tell, for the better. But it would not be unfair to say, surely, as the first generation of free Americans gives way to new leaders and a new age, that this is an author which gives promise of becoming, in the spirited words of the First Continental Congress, "a nation led to greatness by the hand of liberty."

Acknowledgments

MARTHA C. LEISTER, AN ABLE, IMAGINATIVE LIBRARIAN, FOR MANY years directed the Public Documents Department of The Free Library of Philadelphia. She did so with unusual vigor and the most exacting professional standards. There is no help a scholar receives comparable to this. I first used her department in the course of a study of the debates of the First Federal Congress. Later, for some while I was her co-worker in The Free Library, and from observing her thorough, intensive application of what librarians call classification and analysis skills to the formidable materials before her, I came to appreciate the problems—the pleasures, too—of dealing with government publications. To Mrs. Leister and the excellent staff she trained to succeed her, to Jeanne E. Hull the present head, Mrs. Gertrude Scott and Mrs. Yetta Nicoll, I wish to acknowledge a particular and special obligation extending now over more than a decade.

Even more substantial are the many obligations which, in common with everyone else who now studies early American history, I owe to Mr. Julian P. Boyd. Several of these I was at pains to describe in the text of the lectures. But to mention his basic study, *The Declaration of Independence,* and his present imposing masterwork, *The Papers of Thomas Jefferson,* is to do no more than begin the catalogue of his contributions to the understanding of our revolutionary and national periods. His studies include the Wyoming Papers, the Trenton trials, the Galloway plans, Indian treaties, and numerous other aspects of the various problems touched on in these talks, to each of which he has taken his unique gifts of analysis and good sense. In the interests of scholarship, Mr. Boyd read my manuscript before publication, and improved it greatly by suggestions, additions, and corrections. No one else could have helped with such authority, and such a sure hand, and very few would have been so generous.

In 1933, '34, and '35 Dr. Jameson and Dr. E. C. Burnett, with their characteristic kindness to a worker just starting in the field, took pains to show me the Continental Congress papers in The Library of Congress, and talk to me about the various uses that could be made of them. Lately, the National Archives staff has been of direct personal help, far beyond the call of their duties; but again it is the skill and thoroughness with which they have discharged their duties that make the research worker abundantly grateful to them. Particularly, it is a pleasure to acknowledge the friendly assistance of Paul Lewinson and O. W. Holmes, and the inexhaustible patience, energies, and interest of Mr. Harold E. Hufford and Watson G. Caudill to whose immediate charge the papers of the houses of Congress are consigned.

Earle E. Coleman, bibliographer at The Longwood Library, having heard these lectures delivered, still discovered the hardihood to volunteer to assist in the preparation of the manuscript for printing, and saved me from errors I should have been sorry to commit.

Dr. Kenneth M. Setton, Mr. Rudolph Hirsch, Mrs. Neda Westlake, Dean Roy F. Nichols, Professor Robert M. Spiller, and Mr. William McCarthy made the arrangements for delivering these lectures, and the agreeable Philadelphia occasions surrounding them, pleasant and colorful. Dr. Charles W. David and Mr. Thomas R. Adams were responsible for the original invitation to me, for which I had prepared a suitable expression of thanks, but I was forestalled from delivering it by the upsetting circumstances that both of those gentlemen, almost immediately after scheduling my talks, left their posts at the University. I reflected on this with some misgivings, until it was observed that both did appear in the audience to brave the consequences of their decision.

Mr. Barney Chesnick and Edwin Wolf 2nd of The Library Company of Philadelphia, Mr. R. Norris Williams and the staff of The Historical Society of Pennsylvania, the staff of the Washingtoniana Division of the Public Library of Washington, D.C., were generous and efficient in assisting me to study the resources of their important institutions.

Mrs. Joseph Carson, whose extraordinary gifts as a collector have illuminated many parts of the American past, was generous both in the materials and the encouragement she offered. To her, I owe an obligation by no means entirely discharged on the dedicatory page of this little volume—a page designed to memorialize a fellowship to which she invariably made a unique, and a rich, contribution.

After-Words
On Certain Sources

1. The National Archives. From the first day of Independence down to its final establishment in our very own time, the want of a National Archives or National Historical Department was a plague and confusion to American Studies. The story of the founding, finally, of the National Archives is told, in all its struggles, disappointments, and ultimate fulfillment, in the recent volume edited by the late Elizabeth Donnan and Leo F. Stock, *An Historian's World: Selections From the Correspondence of John Franklin Jameson* (Philadelphia, American Philosophical Society, 1956). The volume is a scholar's joy; it renews much of the activity-creating inspiration of Dr. Jameson himself.

The Archives, so lately started, at once by its custodial care and its publications opened up a new era in American scholarship. In its short life as an institution, three successive archivists have guided it from its beginnings to its present premier place among official repositories of nations. Dr. Connor's particular genius was policy, Dr. Buck's was archival theory, Dr. Wayne Grover's is administration. Each seemed to appear in the archivist's office exactly when his gifts were most needed. And the staff they have built up, even with all the difficulties of building and holding a trained staff in Washington in our time, must certainly be counted as able, enlightened, and dedicated a staff as any government bureau anywhere can show.

Every study of government records should start with the *Guide to the Records in the National Archives,* 1948 edition, which describes not only the records, but the problems of keeping them, and the structure, function, and procedure of the government offices that made them, as well. For the period covered by these lectures, four "Record Groups" were particularly important. (1) Record Groups 11, "General Records of the United States Government," is described on pages 30-36 of the *Guide.* (2) The "Continental Congress Records," six feet of them (archives are at least measured when they are too numerous to catalogue), compromise part of Record Group 12, "Department of State, General Records," and are described on pages 222-223. These Continental Congress papers are the small part of the whole collection held back, for reasons more quaint than sensible, by the Department of State when the bulk of the Continental Congress material was transferred in 1903 to The Library of Congress. It is unfortunate that this division of all Charles Thomson's records into two units, one large, one small, housed in two places, was permitted to take place. For the bibliographer, the "six feet" in the National Archives has special importance, for Congress' own copies of their own printings, such as have survived, are here. I think it would be a worthy project to secure a bibliographical analysis of them.

(3) In addition to the *Guide,* the National Archives publishes a more detailed *Preliminary Inventory* of each record group as it is processed. Record Group 46, "Records of the United States Senate," consists of 6,558 *cubic* feet of material, all transferred by December 31, 1949, to the Archives, too late for the 1948 *Guide.* In 1950, *Preliminary Inventory No. 23* described this Senate collection, in 284 pages. I analyze my use of the papers in this Record Group in the footnotes to Lectures II and III, below, and follow the *Preliminary Inventory*'s location scheme. (4) The House of Representatives Papers, which came later to the Archives, will soon be available for scholars. I was permitted to see them and to study the analysis that is being made for the forthcoming preliminary inventory which will describe them.

2. *The Continental Congress Papers in The Library of Congress.* In 1903 the State Department transferred all but six feet of its collection of Continental Congress Papers to the Library of Congress, where it has been available to scholars, but not very much used, ever since. It was available to Evans, Vail, and Cole; it could have solved some of their problems. Only W. C. Ford and his successors as editors of the *Journals,* and Dr. E. C. Burnett made systematic and thorough use of this largest single resource for the history of our Revolutionary period, until Professor Jensen very recently has begun to study them anew. Many scattered items of the

printing history of the years 1774–89 can be combed from the 196 groups of volumes in this collection. The whole enormous mass of materials is described in *Handbook of Manuscripts in the Library of Congress*, 1918, pages 79-90. The State Department had analyzed it more particularly in "Catalogue of the Papers of the Continental Congress," *Bulletin of the Bureau of Rolls . . . No. 1*, Sept., 1893. Earlier, in 1855, a 72-page *Catalogue* had been published by the Department.

3. Shipton's Continuation of Evans. In the text, I have indicated the weaknesses of Sabin's *Bibliotheca Americana*, and Charles Evans' *American Bibliography* in the field of American Documents. This weakness does not exist in *The American Bibliography of Charles Evans, Vol. 13, 1799–1800*, which Mr. Clifford K. Shipton has recently prepared. In this continuation, United States publications for 1799, and for the year of the move to Washington, 1800, are carefully and fully listed. Their Evans numbers are 36467-36598, and 38687-38911. Four items in Mr. Shipton's list are ones I have considered long and hard to try to decide if one of them could be the first government imprint in Washington: no. 38689, because of the careful statement of the imprint; 38690, because Way and Groff describe their new Washington location so particularly; 38737 because it is a Duane 1800 imprint (but I think it must have been printed in Philadelphia); and finally 38813 because of its early date, November 26. I cannot place any of them earlier than the first week's Senate *Journal*, if that first week's *Journal* was delivered as a separate sheet.

4. The Checklist of 1911. One of the most remarkable bibliographies in American Studies, indispensable to anyone who would seriously study the American government or use federal publications for any purpose, is a fat quarto volume of 1707 pages, with this title:

Checklist / of / United States Public / Documents / 1789–1909 / Congressional: to the close of Sixtieth Congress / Departmental: to end of calendar year 1909 / Third Edition / Revised and Enlarged / Volume 1 / Lists of Congressional and Departmental Publications / Compiled under direction of the / Superintendent of Documents / Washington / Government Printing Office / 1911

It is called *Volume 1* because the Superintendent intended to publish as volume 2 an index to the whole work. The second volume, unfortunately, never appeared.

Now this is the work always referred to as the *Checklist of 1911.* It is technically an excellent bibliography, full of excellent technical information about the history of the government.

Its publication story began with John G. Ames, Superintendent of Documents when the Public Documents Office was part of the Interior Department, before it was placed in the Government Printing Office. Ames was the leading authority on federal documents of his period, the best-trained and most skillful workman ever to appear in the field. He it was who compiled the *Comprehensive Index to the Publications of the United States Government, 1881–1893,* which librarians always call simply "Ames," and he was also the one who conceived and started the great *Documents Catalogue* (1893–1940). In 1882, Ames published a catalogue of fifty years' issues by the Congress, called *List of Congressional Documents, 20th to 46th Congress.* It was far superior to anything else for the years it covered. In 1892, he expanded this to a much more ambitious publication, *List of Congressional Documents, 15th to 51st Congress, and of Government Publications containing debates and proceedings of Congress 1st-51st Congress, with miscellaneous lists of public documents, historical and bibliographical notes.* This expanded list came to be known as the *First Checklist.*

Its usefulness exhausted the edition at once, and in three years F. A. Crandall, Ames's successor, issued a still more enlarged and detailed work, the *Second Checklist,* 1895. The work had thus grown during more than a decade to a major project, and in the Superintendent's office a staff was continually adding to it. Superintendents Crandall and Donath regarded it as a vital part of their public service. In 1908 Donath began the publication of supplementary revisions called *Advance Sheets,* 132 of which were distributed before the final publication of the great *Third Checklist* in 1911.

It has never been revised and reissued in a Fourth Checklist. I wish it might be. Its principal value is, of course, retrospective. It is a concise view of the past history it overlooks. An up-to-date edition, including the last fifty years, would be invaluable. Particularly, it would be invaluable because the *Documents Catalogue* was suspended in 1940. The end of this remarkable tool with its twenty-fifth volume is another in the long series of misfortunes that have plagued the field of government publications. Even though substantive improvements have been made in the *Monthly Catalogue* (which is all we have left, now in the era of the government's largest and most important publication period), it is still by no means an adequate substitute for the *Documents Catalogue*. But the government, frequently so prodigal with funds, has always proved a poor supporter of its own housekeeping.

5. *Handbooks and Guides*. The novice in federal government publications may be somewhat repelled at first by the professional librarians' literature on this subject, but he will be assisted if he sustains his interest sufficiently to consult these works:

ALA Committee on Public Documents: *Papers presented at conferences* of the ALA 1933–1942. Chicago (ALA), 1934–38; 1942. 7 Vols.

Boyd, Anne Morris: *United States Government Publications.* 3rd ed., revised by Rae Elizabeth Rips. N. Y., 1949.

Brown, Everett S.: *Manual of Government Publications, United States and Foreign.* N. Y., 1950.

Childs, James Bennett: *Government Documents Bibliography in the United States and Elsewhere.* 3rd ed., Washington, 1942.

Clarke, Edith E.: *Guide to the Use of United States Government Publications.* Boston, 1918.

Hirshberg, Herbert S., and Carl H. Melinat: *Subject Guide to United States Government Publications.* Chicago (ALA), 1947.

Leidy, W. Philip: *A Popular Guide to Government Publications.* N. Y., 1953.

McCanny, James L.: *Government Publications for the Citizen.* N. Y., 1949.

Tompkins, Dorothy C.: *Materials for the Study of Federal Government.* Chicago, 1948.

Winchell, Constance M.: *Guide to Reference Books.* 7th ed., Chicago, 1951. Succeeding Mudge, Isadore Gilbert: *Guide . . .* in four editions; and the originator of this work, Kroeger, Alice Bertha: *Guide . . . ,* 1902, with annual supplements.

Notes

In general, since these were lectures delivered to a professional audience, I tried to indicate in the text the sources of such facts as I was discussing. When the source is thus clearly indicated, I have not made a note that would merely repeat the citation. For example, when I referred plainly to Robert Aitken's "Waste Book," said it was in The Library Company, and then quoted from it, I resisted the scholar's conditioned reflex to write a footnote after the quotation that would say no more than "Aitken, Robert. *Waste Book*. MS Div., PPLC."

And since these were talks about bibliography rather than bibliographies, I have not given Evans, Sabin, and Greely numbers or pages, when I mentioned titles, unless in some special case there seemed to be a special reason for doing so. The nature of the National Archives finding aids, on the other hand, seems to me to make necessary an exact citation of the folder in which a letter in the Senate files, not individually catalogued, is to be found.

I. NOVUS ORDO SECLORUM

1. *A Book Hunter's Holiday,* 106.
2. *Id.,* 145-46.
3. Hunt, Gaillard: *The Seal of the United States, passim.* Ford, W. C., ed.: *Journals of the Continental Congress,* XXII, 338-40. Burnett, E. C., ed.: *Letters of the Members of the Continental Congress,* V, 149-50; VI, 374-75, with citations there. Boyd, J. P., ed.: *The Papers of Thomas Jefferson,* I, 494-97; VI, 426, n.

4. The first time was in 1951, when Dr. Lewis Hanke delivered his original and spirited lectures, *Bartolomé de las Casas, Bookman, Scholar, Propagandist* (Philadelphia, 1952).

5. See, for example, Bemis, S. F.: "Washington's Farewell Address," *Am. Hist. Rev.,* XXXIX (Jan. 1934), 250-68.

6. See, of course, his remarkable notes throughout his *Papers of Thomas Jefferson.* These set the highest standards of historical criticism and editing, certainly, that has been achieved in American studies. And I had in mind also his *The Declaration of Independence, the Evolution of the Text;* and his article, "The Disputed Authorship of the Declaration on the Causes and Necessity for Taking Up Arms, 1775," *Penna. Mag. Hist. and Biog.,* LXXIV (Jan. 1950), 51-73.

7. Sabin, XXVI, 118.

8. *Id.,* IV, 379.

9. *Id.,* no. 15535.

10. *Id.,* no. 15593.

11. The Papers of the Continental Congress, be it noted, were accessible in the Department of State when Sabin, Evans, and P. L. Ford were doing their works, and had even been catalogued in published documents.

12. Walsh, Michael J.: "Contemporary Broadside Editions of the Declaration of Independence," *Harvard Library Bulletin,* III, No. 1 (Winter, 1949), 31-43. His reference to Hays is: Hays, I. Minis: *A Contribution to the Bibliography of the Declaration of Independence,* Phila., 1900.

13. Pollock and Maitland: *The History of English Law,* I, 194. Holdsworth: *A History of English Law,* II, 477, with other references in both these works on the Seal, and on the problem of language in law. *OED,* 1933 ed., notes the analogy to publishing a will, or publishing a judicial sentence, or publishing the banns of marriage. *Black's Law Dictionary,* 1951 ed., remarks with a precision scarcely characteristic of that annoying volume that publication of copies of laws with the purpose of making them easily accessible forms no part of the process of enactment, but that promulgation in some form of proclamation or announcement is preliminary to an enactment's acquiring the force and operation of law. Cases are cited. McLaughlin and Hart, *Cyclopedia of*

American Government, 1949, discusses the matter under the heading "Acts of Congress."

14. The bibliographical notes W. C. Ford wrote are nothing more, for the most part, than a reprinting of his brother P. L. Ford's 1888 bibliography of Continental Congress publications, with all the extraneous material still retained. For example, I find only ten official publications of the First Congress of 1774, but P. L. Ford listed forty-two. Unquestionably, in this respect the *Journals* are deficient. W. C. Ford apparently did not even look at (for he did not describe) the copies of printings in the part of the Congress papers retained at the State Department. The citations by volume and pages of the bibliographical notes in the *Journals* is as follows:

I, 127-36	XV, 1451-63	XXVII, 719-24
III, 507-16	XVIII, 1233-37	XXIX, 915-31
VI, 1117-28	XXI, 1199-1203	XXXI, 957-69
IX, 1081-89	XXIII, 885-89	XXXIII, 753-57
XII, 1281-89	XXV, 983-91	XXXIV, 631-36

15. The *Association* is properly regarded, also, as the first national law, or at least a quasi law. For it applied not just to the signers as a voluntary pledge, but to "all persons," and enforcement provisions embraced, beyond merchants and citizens, masters of American vessels in foreign ports, embraced even punitive actions against whole provinces. See Schlesinger, A. M.: *The Colonial Merchants and the American Revolution,* 421-29, *et passim.*

16. The manuscript agreement of secrecy, Nov. 9, 1775, signed by eighty-seven delegates from 1775 to 1777 including fifty of the Signers of the Declaration of Independence, is in the MS Division, Library of Congress.

17. Burnett: *Letters,* I, 84. No. 120.

18. *Id.,* 90. No. 125.

19. *Id.,* 83. No. 118.

20. *Id.,* 84. No. 120.

21. For Bradfords, see Wallace, John W.: *An Old Philadelphian* (1884) ; Hildeburn, C. R.: *A Century of Printing; the Issues of the Press of Pennsylvania, 1685–1784* (1885) ; *Penna. Mag. Hist. and Biog.,* XXI, 170-76; 448.

22. Burnett: *Letters*, I, 83. No. 117.

23. Boyd: "Disputed Authorship," *cit. sup.*, n. 6. And see his full discussion of the same subject in *Jefferson Papers*, I, 187-218.

24. Boyd: *Jefferson Papers*, I, 299-308. In 1819, Jefferson wrote another note, which says [italics mine]: "the Declaration thus signed on the 4th. *on paper* was engrossed on parchment, & signed again on the 2d. of Aug." *Id.*, 301.

25. *Id.*, 315. And for the significance of the word "present" in "every member present except Mr. Dickinson," see *id.*, 328, n. 14.

26. Burnett: *Letters*, I, 527. Ryden, G. H., ed.: *Letters to and From Caesar Rodney*, 94-5.

27. Burnett: *Letters*, I, 528-29. The order is in the "Rough Journal" only, not in the "Corrected Journal." *Authenticated* meant simply signed by the president and secretary, Hancock and Thomson. If a manuscript copy was authenticated before the printing, it must have been the Committee of Five manuscript, which suggests that a signing at least by Hancock and Thomson took place. But Jefferson would never have meant this when he said "signed by all the members present."

28. Ford: *Journals*, V, 555. On receipt of this impressive order, Dunlap and Claypoole went before Magistrate Gibson, and swore this oath (*Journals*, VI, 1123):

We and each of us do swear that we will deliver all the copies of "the articles of confederation" which we shall print together with the copy sheet to the Secretary of Congress and that we will not disclose either directly or indirectly the contents of the said confederation.

                                                    John Dunlap
Philadelphia July 13, 1776   David C. Claypoole
Sworn to before me
          John Gibson

29. Boyd: *Jefferson Papers*, I, 307. Boyd: *Declaration of Independence*, 40-1, 46.

30. Boyd: *Jefferson Papers*, I, 306-8.

31. *Id.*, 308.

32. Burnett: *Letters,* II, 1. No. 1.
33. *Id.,* 5, 7-8. Nos. 8, 12.
34. I delivered this lecture, with its hopeful suggestion that something else might turn up, on April 19, 1956. On the following July 4, a fifteenth copy of the Dunlap broadside, owned by the University of Virginia, was put on display at Monticello. *The New York Times* of July 5, 1956, contained this account of its discovery and provenance:

The fifteenth [copy] came from an Albany attic, a battered prize in a packet of old letters and documents. The broadside was dirty and some of the type imprint was missing. A large piece was missing from the upper left corner and a torn section had been crudely repaired with a patch of linen.

It had been trimmed to narrow margins, very likely the work of an owner who treasured the copy sufficiently to have it framed.

The broadside was bought by the Charles E. Tuttle Company, publishers and booksellers of Rutland, Vt., for restoration.

The problem was handed to Harold Tribolet, manager of the hand bindery of the R. R. Donnelley & Sons Company in Chicago. Restoration experts on Mr. Tribolet's staff, after study, said the copy was disintegrating, but not hopeless of salvage.

Searches for the missing piece had failed, so the book surgeons decided on a "graft."

They reproduced a similar portion of a well-preserved copy in the Harvard University Library.

Among the bindery's stock of antique paper was found a paper that had virtually the identical thickness, color, texture and ink-taking characteristics of the aged broadside.

An ink was then compounded to match Dunlap's 1776 batch. In the next step, the text was printed on the substitute for the missing piece. The grafting operation was completed through a "knitting" process.

When all restorations were finished the document had the appearance of a mellow, well-preserved 180-year-old.

The Tuttle company sold the work to David Randall, a rare-book expert. He in turn sold the broadside "for something under $10,000" to friends of the University of Virginia.

Contributors to the purchase for the university were C. Waller Barrett, a New York alumnus; the Thomas Jefferson Memorial Foundation and the McGregor Fund, established by the late Tracy W. McGregor of Detroit.

II. E PLURIBUS UNUM

1. See Ford, P. L.: *Bibliography and Reference History of . . . the Constitution,* Brooklyn, 1888. Ford, P. L.: *Pamphlets on The Constitution,* Brooklyn, 1888. Farrand, Max: *Records of the Federal Convention,* rev. ed., New Haven, 1937. And [Boyd, J. P.:] *The Constitution of the United States,* a bibliographical catalogue of a definitive exhibition held at The Historical Society of Pennsylvania in 1937.

2. Farrand: *Records,* I, xii-xiii.

3. [Boyd, J. P.:] *The Constitution,* 22-3. No. 87.

4. *Journals,* XXXIII, 753, 760-62.

5. Farrand: *Records,* II, 623, 634; III, 81.

6. Fitzpatrick, John C.: *The Writings of George Washington,* vol. 29, 276-77.

7. See the bibliographical notes in the *Journals,* cited in n. 14 to Lecture I, above.

8. Probably for Flower's own Pennsylvania regiment, since Col. Flower (Burnett calls him Flowers) was not Commissary General of Continental forces until 1778.

9. I add Vattel, because C. W. F. Dumas from The Hague had sent Franklin a copy of his work in the fall of 1775, and Franklin attached great importance to receiving it, "when the circumstances of a rising State make it frequently necessary to consult the law of nations." Wharton, *Rev. Dipl. Corresp.,* II, 64-67. Cole's description of the Church copy of the Articles is in his *Catalogue of . . . Church,* V, 130.

10. ". . . who afterwards distinguished himself at the taking of Stoney Point . . ." Whitehead, James L., ed.: "The Autobiography of Peter S. DuPonceau," *Penna. Mag. Hist. and Biog.,* LXIII, Nos. 2, 3, 4, Apr., Jly., Oct., 1939, 189-227; 311-43; 432-61. At p. 215.

11. Only legends also were many other of the anecdotes of Du-Ponceau's nearsightedness and absent-mindedness, but they had a basis in certain true episodes: his bowing to his own image in a mirror; his excited reporting of a line of red petticoats hanging out to dry as a body of British soldiers. These he describes himself in an autobiographical letter: *Penna. Mag. Hist. and Biog.*, *cit. sup.*, 457-59.

12. DuPonceau's own account of his part in the preparation of the manual, for which he received $400 additional pay from Congress, is in his "Autobiography," *cit. sup.*, 215-16.

13. *Journals*, XIII, 384-85. March 29, 1779. Letter of Board of War to Congress, April 2, 1779, praising Fleury, Walker, L'Enfant, and DuPonceau, and appointing L'Enfant captain, retroactively, *id.*, 411-12. Resolution of thanks to von Steuben, April 5, 420. On April 16, Congress voted $1,000 for Fleury, $600 for Walker, $500 for L'Enfant, $400 for DuPonceau, and $4,000 for von Steuben himself. *Id.*, 459.

14. The development of Congress' committees, reliance on them, and congressional willingness to give committees independent budgets and powers, an uneven development, can be traced through Burnett: *The Continental Congress*, esp. p. 118 f., and in Sanders, J. B.: *Evolution of Executive Departments of the Continental Congress*, Chapel Hill, 1935.

15. Butterfield, L. H.: "Elder John Leland." *Amer. Antiq. Soc., Proceedings*, Oct., 1952, 193.

16. The *Preliminary Inventory* of the House Records is not yet available, but is in preparation. It will serve as an introduction to the collection when it appears.

17. *Preliminary Inventory of the Records of the United States Senate*, 1950, prepared by Harold E. Hufford and Watson G. Caudill, is a description of the Senate Records, in the excellent standard form worked out by the Archives staff. All my citations of the Senate Records refer to the record groups by index numbers in this inventory, which are the call numbers to be used in examining the papers at the National Archives.

18. Sen 1D-A1. That is, Senate Papers, 1 [First Congress] D [records of the Office of the Secretary] — A1, a specific group, this one consisting of letters on fiscal estimates and expenditures of the first

session. Within this group, each letter or document is not separately catalogued or indexed, but is placed in a chronological arrangement.

In 1792, the Civil List provided these salaries for the two legislative offices, and these contingent expenses:

Secretary of Senate	$1,896	Clerk of House	$1,896
First Clerk	1,095	Principal Clerk	1,104
Second Clerk	500	Engrossing Clerk	396
Extra Clerk	320	Engrossing Clerk	502
Doorkeeper	794	Chaplain	272
Assistant Doorkeeper	552	Sgt. at Arms	792
Contingent Expenses	4,093	Doorkeeper	827
		Assistant Doorkeeper	574
		Contingent Expenses	4,004

In 1816, the salaries of the Secretary and Clerk were raised to $2,500 each, and other salaries proportionately. *American State Papers, Miscellaneous,* I, 59; II, 299-300.

19. Sen 1D-A3. "A3" is a group indexed as "printing and stationery for the Senate, together with contracts."

20. *Id.*

21. *Id.*

22. *Id.*

23. *Id.*

24. *Id.*

25. *Id.*

26. *Id.*

27. *Id.*

28. See, e.g., Evans, 22199, 22200.

29. Sen 1D-A3.

30. Evans, 22193. Mr. Edwin Wolf 2nd described a set of nine separate folio laws (slip laws) of 1791 in the McAllister Collection, Library Company of Philadelphia, in the *Annual Report* of that institution for the year 1955, pp. 11-12. Each is signed by Secretary Jefferson. One of them is not an act at all, but a resolution addressing the National Assembly of France in acknowledgment of the tribute it had paid to Benjamin Franklin following his death. Recording of laws in books by the State Department ceased by

act of Congress in 1838. Publication in newspapers ceased by act
of Congress in 1875.

31. Sen 1D-A4; 2D-A3; 3D-A2.

32. Sen 1D-A3. Of special interest is a letter from Moreau de
St. Mery to Otis, Dec. 26, 1794. Sen 3D-A1.

33. Sen 1D-A3.

34. Evans, 22987.

35. H. Remsen Jr. to S. A. Otis, Dec. 30, 1790. Sen 1D-A4.

36. See, among others, White, Leonard D.: *The Federalists,* 505-6.

37. Sen 1D-A4.

38. Sen 2D-A4.

39. Sen 3D-A1.

40. Sen 3D-A1. John Fenno to S. A. Otis, March 1, 1795.

41. J. W. Fenno to S. A. Otis, May 31, 1800. Sen 6D-A3.

42. John Fenno to S. A. Otis, Dec. 5, 1797. Sen 5D-A2.

43. Sen 5D-A2.

44. H. Remsen Jr. to S. A. Otis, Nov. 2, 1791. Sen 2D-A3.

45. Sen 6D-A3.

46. Timothy Pickering to S. A. Otis, Jan. 26, 1797. Sen 4D-A4.

47. John Fenno to Otis, Feb. 28, 1797. Sen 4D-A4.

48. In Sen 5C-A1 is the manuscript record of the contempt proceeding of the Senate against Duane, kept by the Secretary and his
clerks. The *Annals* of Congress give the debates and the record.
And see Miller, John C.: *Crisis in Freedom: The Alien and Sedition Acts;* Smith, James Morton: *Freedom's Fetters: The Alien and
Sedition Laws and American Civil Liberties;* and the same writer's
account of Duane before the Senate: "The Aurora and The Alien
and Sedition Laws. Part II: The Editorship of William Duane,"
Penna. Mag. Hist. and Biog., LXXVII, No. 2 (Apr. 1953), 123-55.

49. E.g., Sen 4D-A4.

50. Evans, 27884, 27885.

51. Evans, 24946.

52. Evans, 26343.

53. Evans, 27930-31.

54. See, for a discussion of this much-discussed issue, Charles,
Joseph: "The Jay Treaty," *William and Mary Quarterly,* 3rd ser.,
XII, No. 4 (Oct., 1955), 581-630, esp. 595. References there.

55. Evans, 31412.

56. *Id.*, 27978.
57. *Id.*, 31356.
58. *Id.*, 31402.
59. *Id.*, 31436-31442.
60. *Id.*, 31445.
61. *Id.*, 31446.
62. *Id.*, 31461.
63. *Id.*, 32951-52.
64. *Id.*, 33040.
65. *Id.*, 33042.
66. *Id.*, 33043.
67. *Id.*, 33075.
68. *Id.*, 33089.
69. *Id.*, 33096.
70. *Id.*, 34781.
71. *Id.*, 34822.
72. *Id.*, 34837.
73. *Id.*, 34841.
74. *Id.*, 34858-59.
75. Adams, *Works*, IX, 51. White, *The Federalists*, 506.
76. George Hyde to John Dempsie, Oct. 9, 1800. Sen 6D-A3.

III. ANNUIT COEPTIS

1. Columbia Historical Society, *Records,* IV, 1901. 32-74.
2. *Id.,* 68.
3. Clark, Allen C.: "General Roger Chew Weightman," Col. Hist. Soc., *Records,* XXII, 1919, 62-104; same author: "Joseph C. Gales, Jr.," *id.,* XXIII, 86-144; same author: "Daniel Rapine," *id.,* XXV, 194-215. McMurtrie, Douglas C.: *History of Printing in the United States,* II, 254-75. Proctor, John Clagett: "Washington Past and Present," *Sunday Star,* Washington, March 9, 1930, March 16, 1930. Bryan, Wilhelmus Bogart: *A History of the National Capital,* I, 383, 435-37, 595-96, 598. [Crew, H. W.]: *Centennial History of the City of Washington, D.C.* (Dayton, Ohio, 1892) , 441-46.
4. Caldwell, L. K.: *The Administrative Theories of Hamilton & Jefferson* (Chicago, 1944), 84 ff., 239 ff. White: *The Federalists,*

esp. 507 ff.; *The Jeffersonians, passim.* Kenyon, Cecelia M.: "Men of Little Faith: The Anti-Federalists on the Nature of Representative Government," *William and Mary Quarterly,* 3rd ser., XII, No. 1 (Jan. 1955), 3-43.

5. Morison, Samuel Eliot: *The Life and Letters of Harrison Gray Otis, Federalist,* I, 203, n., *et passim.*

6. Sen 7D-A4.

7. Feb. 19, 1802. Sen 7D-A4.

8. Apr. 15, 1802. Sen 7D-A4.

9. Apr. 21, 1802. Sen 7D-A4.

10. Mar. 12, 1802. Sen 7D-A4.

11. May 1, 1802. Sen 7D-A4.

12. Jan. 1, 1804. Sen 8D-A3.

13. Dec. 14, 1804. Sen 8D-A3.

14. Jan. 1, 1804. Sen 8D-A3.

15. Sen 8D-B1.

16. Marsh, Philip M.: "John Beckley, Mystery Man of the Early Jeffersonians," *Penna. Mag. Hist. and Biog.,* LXXII, No. 1 (Jan., 1948), 54-69. And see Faÿ, Bernard: *The Two Franklins,* for the Bache-Fenno story.

17. Dec. 20, 1805. Sen 9D-A2.

18. Sen 9D-A2.

19. R. C. Weightman for William Duane, to S. A. Otis, Dec. 8, 1806. Sen 9D-A2.

20. March 3, 1807. Sen 9D-A2.

21. May 31, 1807. Sen 10D-A3.

22. *Id.*

23. Jan. 17, 1805. Sen 8D-A3.

24. Clark: "Weightman," Col. Hist. Soc. *Records,* XXII, 62-104.

25. May 31, 1807. Sen 10D-A3.

26. Endorsement June 8, 1808, by Otis on Weightman's letter of May 31, *loc. cit.*

27. Sen 10D-A3, *et seq.*

28. Sen 10D-A3, *bis; et al.*

29. May 31, 1807; Mar. 28, 1808. Sen 10D-A3.

30. Nov. 25, 1808. Sen 10D-A3.

31. Sen 11D-A3: bills Dec. 1809, Jan. 1811, Feb. 1811, etc.

32. Jan. 12, 1811. Sen 11D-A3.

33. A note promising to pay given by Magruder is in Mrs. Joseph Carson's collection.

34. Jan. 20, 1812; March 10, 1812. Sen 12D-A3.

35. *Checklist*, 1052.

36. June 29, 1811. Sen 12A-J2.

37. Nov. 8, 1811. Sen 12D-A3.

38. Feb. 18, 1811. Sen 11D-A3.

39. Nov. 21, 1812. Sen 12D-A3; and *cf.* Dec. 5, 1812: "I have not copy enough for more than *five* pages of the Journal. Today's proceedings, when rec^d., may probably make out the half-sheet." Sen 12D-A3.

40. Jan. 17, 1812. Sen 12D-A3.

41. Dec. 8, 1812. Sen 12D-A3.

42. Dec. 9, 1812. Sen 12D-A3.

43. Clark: "Weightman," *cit. sup.*

44. E.g., bill of Feb., 1811. Sen 11D-A3.

45. Jan. 1811. Sen 11D-A3.

46. Mar. 19, 1812. Sen 12D-A3.

47. E.g., Feb. 11, 1811. Sen 11D-A3.

48. Feb. 12, 1814. Sen 13D-A3.

49. Apr. 22, 1812. Sen 12D-A1.

50. Treasury warrant, Jan. 15, 1814. Sen 13D-A1.

51. Jan. 22, 1810. Sen 11A-D4.

52. July 2, 1813. Sen 13D-A3.

53. E.g., July 26, 1813. Sen 13D-A3.

54. Weightman to Otis, Feb. 22, 1813, Sen 13D-A3.

55. Aug. 1, 1813; July 2, 1813. Sen 13D-A3.

56. Aug. 1, 1813, *bis*. Sen 13D-A3.

57. June 8, 1813. Sen 13D-A3.

58. Jan. 7, 1814. Sen 13D-A3; and Greely's listings for this year.

59. Jan. 29, 1814. Sen 13D-A3.

60. Feb. 1, 1814. Sen 13D-A3.

61. Jan. 29, 1814. Sen 13D-A3.

62. Sen 13D-A3.

Index

163